The Seven Contemplations of Insight

Publisher's Note

This book was prepared under the guidance of the Venerable Mātara Śri Ñāṇārāma Mahāthera, widely recognized as one of Sri Lanka's outstanding meditation masters of recent times. Born in the southern town of Mātara in 1901, he received novice ordination (*pabbajjā*) in 1917 and higher ordination (*upasampadā*) in 1922. From 1967 until his death in 1992 he was the resident meditation master of the Nissaraṇa Vanaya Hermitage at Mītirigala, an austere monastery devoted to the strict meditative life. He also served as the head master (*pradhanācārya*) of the Śri Kalyāṇi Yogāśrama Association, a Buddhist monastic organization of the forest tradition comprising more than a hundred branch monasteries in Sri Lanka. The Sri Lanka Rāmañña Mahānikāya conferred on him the honorary title of chief preceptor (*mahopādhyāya*). His numerous publications in Sinhala include *Sapta Viśuddhiya-hā-Vidarśanā-gñāṇa, Samatha-Vidarśanā Bhāvanā Mārgaya, Ānāpānasati Bhāvanā*, and *Vidarśanā Parapura*. (The first of these is published by the BPS in English translation under the title *The Seven Stages of Purification and the Insight Knowledges*.) He was also a prolific author of Buddhist poetry in Sinhala, Pāli, and Sanskrit.

The Seven Contemplations of Insight

A Treatise on Insight Meditation

Prepared under the guidance of
Venerable Mātara
Śri Ñāṇārāma Mahāthera

by one of his pupil-monks
based on a treatise of
the Venerable Mahāthera

English translation from the Sinhala by
A.G.S. Kariyawasam

Buddhist Publication Society
Kandy • Sri Lanka

First published in 1997

Buddhist Publication Society
P.O. Box 61
54, Sangharaja Mawatha
Kandy, Sri Lanka

Originally published in Sinhala as *Sat Anupassanā* by Mithra Wettimuny (1991).

ISBN 955-24-0124-0

Typeset at the BPS

Printed in Sri Lanka by
Karunaratne & Sons Ltd.
Colombo 10

Contents

Abbreviations

A.	Aṅguttara Nikāya (PTS)
AA.	Aṅguttara Nikāya Aṭṭhakathā (SHB)
AṬ.	Aṅguttara Nikāya Ṭikā (BCS)
BCS	Burmese script Chaṭṭha Saṅgāyanā ed.
CNid.	Cūlaniddesa (Sinhala script Buddhajayanti ed.)
D.	Dīgha Nikāya (PTS)
DA.	Dīgha Nikāya Aṭṭhakathā (SHB)
DṬ.	Dīgha Nikāya Ṭikā (SHB)
Dhp.	Dhammapada (by verse)
It.	Itivuttaka (PTS)
ItA.	Itivuttaka Aṭṭhakathā (SHB)
KhuA.	Khuddakapāṭha Aṭṭhakathā (SHB)
M.	Majjhima Nikāya (PTS)
MA.	Majjhima Nikāya Aṭṭhakathā (SHB)
Pm.	Paṭisambhidāmagga (PTS)
PmA.	Paṭisambhidāmagga Aṭṭhakathā (SHB)
PTS	Pali Text Society
Pug.	Puggalapaññatti (PTS)
S.	Saṁyutta Nikāya (PTS)
SA.	Saṁyutta Nikāya Aṭṭhakathā (SHB)
Sn.	Suttanipāta (by verse)
SHB	Sinhala script Simon Hewavitarne Bequest ed.
Thag.	Theragāthā (by verse)
Ud.	Udāna (PTS)
Vism.	Visuddhimagga (chapter and paragraph of the translation by Bhikkhu Ñāṇamoli, *The Path of Purification)*
VismṬ.	Visuddhimagga Ṭikā i: Sinhala script ed. (Byron Senaviratne) ii: BSC ed.

Message

Most Venerable Paṇḍita
Kaḍawädduwe Śrī Jinavaṁsa Mahāthera

Founder-Patron,
Śrī Kalyāṇi Yogāśrama Association

> Thus, Lord, even though many diverse forms perceptible by the eye come within the range of sight of a monk whose mind has been fully liberated thus … he also sees their dissolution.
>
> Mahāvagga (Vinaya i,184)

The life story of the Venerable Soṇa Thera, one of the prominent disciples of the Buddha, is quite a variegated one on the right approach to the practice of meditation. As a layman Soṇa had led a life of extreme luxury. He was brought up in such comfort, it is said, that hair had grown on the soles of his feet. He had renounced all this luxury and entered the Order, but though he applied himself vigorously to his meditation practice he still could not attain arahantship. Finally, thinking that he must be unsuited to the monkhood, he decided to disrobe and return to the household life.

The Buddha came to know of his decision and paid him a visit. He taught the Venerable Soṇa the simile of the lute. Just as a lute can be played only when its strings are neither too tight nor too loose but in perfect balance, so spiritual progress on the path of meditation requires proper balance of the five spiritual faculties: of faith with wisdom, and energy with concentration, mindfulness acting as the supervisor. In the Venerable Soṇa's case the faculty of energy was in excess, and therefore his meditation had not brought forth fruit.

By following the Buddha's instruction and bringing the faculties into harmony, the Venerable Soṇa soon attained arahantship. After reaching the goal he came to the Master and delivered an inspiring address in which he described the nature of the arahant's mind. The epigram at the beginning of this Message is part of that description, showing how the arahant's mind responds to sense objects. Since the arahant sees the dissolution of all sense objects, none of them can get a foothold in his mind.

Let us too develop our own minds to that exalted level. This will free us from the burdens and sufferings of life and finally enable us to experience true deliverance and peace of heart. We have spent enough time wandering mournfully through the cycle of birth and death, burdening the mind with all the useless sense objects demanded by the defilements, just as a trader loads his caravan with merchandise. Let us now prepare ourselves to cast off this burden. We should aim to reach the domain of the noble ones by following the path to free our minds from the deadweight of obstructive passions and desires. That is the fruit of meditation.

As we constantly engage ourselves in our march towards peace, our "pilgrim's progress," let us be able to rejoice by looking at our own forward march. We should not hold to any suffering but should strive to cast off all suffering by its total extirpation. Although we may still be surrounded by suffering, we can be content that we are gradually progressing towards the state where there is no more suffering, cutting off suffering along the way. Let us be constantly mindful of this "pilgrim's progress," for that will surely lead us to the attainment of our life's purpose.

A lighted lamp, wherever it is placed, dispels the darkness and spreads light, illuminating all objects in its range. The change of location makes no difference, for the lamp shines everywhere alike and does not discriminate one dark place from another. Let us be like inextinguishable lamps. First we must illuminate ourselves by realizing the ultimate bliss of the inextinguishable light. Then, out of compassion, we should render this glorious achievement accessible to as many beings as possible. Let our pilgrim's progress, undertaken with this twofold objective in view, proceed from light to light.

In accordance with this Buddhist virtue of compassion, and under the benign guidance of our most revered chief preceptor, the Most Venerable Ñāṇārāma Mahāthera, one of his many devoted pupils has compiled this book on the seven contemplations of insight. I hope and wish that this book will serve as a light for many pilgrims on their journey towards the goal.

May the Dhamma be understood correctly!

KAḌAWÄDDUWE JINAVAṀSA THERA

Gunawardhana Yogāśrama Centre
Galduwa, Kahawa
Sri Lanka

Foreword

Ven. Nāuyane Ariyadhamma Mahāthera
Hony. Registrar,
Śrī Kalyāṇi Yogāśrama Association

The omniscient Buddha declared Nibbāna to be the highest bliss because all other so-called pleasures and comforts are impermanent and mixed with suffering. Insight meditation is the sole way, the unequalled path, leading to the eternal bliss of Nibbāna. We often hear the phrase "the thousandfold path of stream-entry," which implies that there are a thousand approaches to entering the path of stream-entry. Therefore it should be understood that numerous methods of insight meditation are available for attaining the peace of Nibbāna. The present treatise, *The Seven Contemplations of Insight*, draws our attention to this rich diversity of methods.

This book has been compiled by combining the sermons and other instructions of the late Venerable Mātara Śrī Ñāṇārāma Mahāthera, the rich discourses contained in the Sutta Piṭaka, and reports on the actual experiences of insight meditators. The skilful manner in which this treatise has been composed is highly commendable: by collecting various modes of insight meditation and relevant information from the Pāli Canon and commentaries, it is comparable to a necklace made by beading gold and precious gems. As a research study, this book is invaluable. Intelligent readers will find that to read it repeatedly and understand its core message is a successful insight meditation in itself.

The compilation has been made by one of the late Mahāthera's numerous pupils, who had practised meditation under him for many years and who has proven his ability as a gifted preacher and writer. Within this book the Buddha's message of mind development and insight has been recorded with admirable lucidity. The Venerable Compiler has offered a magnificent gift of Dhamma by compiling such an important treatise. Let me wish him the fulfilment of all his good wishes. May he obtain wisdom as deep as that of the Arahant Sāriputta, the Buddha's chief disciple.

The late Venerable Chief Preceptor, by rendering his excellent guidance to the present work, had shown the sole way to deliverance. Thereby he has enabled those with sufficient supporting conditions to realize Nibbāna in this very life, and those who have not completed the perfections to reach Nibbāna in a future life. May there be more great masters of his calibre to uphold the message of the Enlightened One!

May the Buddha's Teaching be firmly established in the world for a long time to come.

NĀUYANE ARIYADHAMMA THERA

Gunawardhana Yogāśrama Centre
Galduwa, Kahawa
Sri Lanka

Compiler's Preface

In 1981 our teacher, the Most Venerable Mātara Śrī Ñāṇārāma Mahāthera, delivered a series of discourses on "the eighteen principal insights" (*aṭṭhārasa mahāvipassanā*) for the benefit of the meditating monks at his monastery, the Nissaraṇa Vanaya Hermitage, at Mītirigala. These discourses brought to light an ancient system of insight meditation comprising eighteen insights, which had received only scant attention in Buddhist literature since the age of the great commentators. Fortunately these lectures were recorded. The other meditators who listened to the tapes were highly benefited by the Master's discourses and thus the tapes became very popular.

Portions of the talks were translated into English for the Western bhikkhus residing at our monastery, several of whom proposed having the entire series translated into English and published in book form. The Venerable Master was agreeable to this proposal. However, rather than simply transcribe his extemporaneous oral discourses, he preferred to compose a fresh book giving extensive coverage to all the eighteen insights, using as a basis the canonical and post-canonical texts as well as the actual experiences of present-day meditators. When the original text was finished several attempts were made to have it translated into English, but for various reasons none succeeded.

In the meantime it was decided to revise the original text on a broader basis. Accordingly, the ancient treatises as well as modern works on meditation were further scrutinized, and simultaneously research was carried out on the practical experiences and observations of senior meditators. As a result the range of information on the principal insights increased significantly. At the same time various problems arose in resolving apparent contradictions in the interpretations of the insights found in the commentarial literature. In order to break this deadlock, it was decided that rather than attempt to treat all eighteen insights in a comprehensive manner, the book would describe the first seven contemplations extensively and would deal with the other eleven insights only briefly in an appendix. As the first seven contemplations already formed a distinct set, the challenge of examining them in detail promised to be sufficiently rewarding. It is thus that the present book gradually took shape.

While the book was evolving over the years, our Venerable Teacher, who was then in his eighties, grew physically weaker and more infirm. Because it had become too difficult for him to collect the relevant passages from the scriptures and to write the book, these tasks devolved upon us, his pupils. We took up this responsibility in constant consultation with our teacher, seeking his advice at every crucial turn, and at the end we submitted the entire manuscript to him for his perusal and final approval.

The main purpose of this book is to offer an analysis and clarification of the "seven contemplations of insight" (*sattānupassanā*), a model of the path of Buddhist meditation frequently referred to in the Pāli commentaries. We have focused on the pragmatic side of this model, but at the same time we have tried to be responsive to the theoretical explanations found in the Pāli source material. The work draws extensively upon the Buddha's discourses from the Sutta Piṭaka, upon exegetical works such as the *Paṭisambhidāmagga* and the *Visuddhimagga*, and upon the Venerable Master's own long-time experience of meditation, both as practitioner and teacher. We have also drawn upon the meditation experiences and explanations of some of the master's pupils. Though our approach is generally practical, we have included discussions of a few controversial points relating to the theoretical foundations of meditation.

A large body of footnotes has been included. These are

intended to serve three main purposes: to clarify obscure points in the basic text; to provide references and signposts for further investigation; and to offer practical hints to the meditator. If the reader finds it distracting to refer to the notes while reading the main body of the exposition, he or she may read the main text first and then refer to the notes on a later occasion. The treatise itself, we hope, strikes a happy balance between practical guidance and theoretical explanation. Although we have tried to keep the presentation clear and simple, owing to the intrinsic depth and difficulty of the points being discussed and the need to be concise the exposition may at times veer towards the abstruse. Readers who find themselves out of their element amidst these doctrinal digressions may simply skip over them and pick up the thread of the practical discussion where it resumes, rarely more than a few paragraphs later. Digressive points raised in the body of the work that required fuller separate treatment have been dealt with in appendices.

While the relative beginner to Buddhist insight meditation may find useful guidance in this book, we recognize that it will be more meaningful for the experienced meditator who is also conversant with the canonical texts. We hope it will be found especially illuminating by those involved in the teaching of insight meditation.

The present work should go far in rekindling an interest in the seven contemplations, which in recent times have fallen into neglect. To our knowledge there is no other work available in print which analyses the seven contemplations so thoroughly. Thus this book serves to fill a major gap in our understanding of the stages of meditative realization. Yet, even in this work, the seven contemplations have been elucidated from within a limited framework. If a broader perspective had been adopted they might have been explained still more extensively and profoundly. And if all the sundry contemplations referred to by the Buddha in the suttas were to be explored systematically, in all their implications, a separate and much larger volume would be required. We hope that, despite its limitations, the present book, compiled under the supervision of one of our age's best qualified meditation masters, may still prove beneficial to meditators in search of authoritative guidance in treading the higher ranges of the path.

* * *

For us it was a source of immense pleasure that we could issue the original Sinhala edition of this book in time for our Venerable Teacher's 90th birthday celebration on 11 December 1991. The book was offered to him as a fitting tribute to one who, during his long and fruitful life in the Sangha, shone like a bright lamp illuminating the Buddha Sāsana in Sri Lanka for many decades. His demise on 30 April 1992, a month after the second edition appeared, was a great loss to all of his pupils personally as well as to the Sāsana.

Many people, both monks and laity, assisted us in different ways in the production of this book. The first and foremost among these was our Venerable Master himself, who despite his physical ailments was always ready to give us his invaluable guidance and blessings, helping us in every possible manner. For his compassionate contribution we are extremely grateful, and we hope this volume will stand as a monument to his revered memory.

More than forty-five years ago, with the Most Venerable Ñāṇārāma Mahāthera as the head master, the Śrī Kalyāṇi Yogāśrama Association was founded for the purpose of reviving the practice of the Buddha's Teaching in this present degenerate age. This organization, which now comprises more than a hundred branch monasteries in the forest tradition, was founded by the Most Venerable Kaḍawädduwe Śrī Jinavaṁsa Mahāthera, who for many years has guided its affairs with great success. When the original Sinhala edition was being prepared he had given us his unreserved encouragement and contributed an inspiring message, for which we express our respectful thanks.

We also thank the indefatigable honorary registrar of the Association, Ven. Nāuyane Ariyadhamma Mahāthera, a prominent meditation teacher and popular preacher, who, despite his many religious duties, had read through the original manuscript, corrected some errors, and provided a foreword. We recall too the enthusiastic and dedicated patronage afforded us by Mr. Mithra Wettimuny, who as a pupil and benefactor of the Venerable Master undertook without hesitation the printing and publication of the Sinhala edition of this work for free distribution, in the spirit of a truly munificent devotee of the Dhamma.

The Buddhist Publication Society of Kandy is to be applauded for its efforts in having the Sinhala text translated and published in English, so that the precious Dhamma contained in this treatise might reach a wide circle of readers beyond the shores of Sri Lanka. Special appreciation is extended to Mr. A.G.S. Kariyawasam, Assistant Editor of the Society, for an exceptionally fine translation, which required a rare combination of talents: excellent knowledge of Sinhala and Pāli, a fluent English literary style, and keen understanding of the Dhamma. We also thank Susan Jootla, a long-time American Buddhist, who typed the handwritten manuscript of the translation into computer format as an expression of her own devotion to the Dhamma.

Many other people, too numerous to mention by name, helped us in various ways to bring this work to light both in the original Sinhala edition as well as in this English translation. To all of them we extend our grateful thanks.

Despite our best efforts, there may have crept into this book errors of omission and commission. For these, we take full responsibility and humbly beg the pardon of our virtuous teachers as well as of the reader.

The Buddha's constant injunction to his disciples was to develop insight knowledge diligently, "like one whose head or clothing is in flames," in order to achieve liberation from the fearful suffering involved in the cycle of birth and death. Therefore, if anyone who reads this book is inspired thereby to strive for that noble goal, or if anyone already involved in the practice is helped by this book to achieve success, we can be overjoyed that our efforts have borne fruit in ample measure.

May all beings share in any merits we may have acquired in preparing this book for publication, a task that was undertaken for the sole purpose of offering the priceless gift of the Dhamma. May all beings develop insight knowledge and realize the Truth!

THE COMPILER

Namo tassa bhagavato arahato sammāsambuddhassa

Introduction

The Path of Insight

People everywhere are constantly engaged in a strenuous attempt to achieve happiness and release from suffering, yet despite such effort they repeatedly fail to arrive at their goal. In the end they are left with nothing but frustration, misery, and a feeling of inward emptiness. "Alas!" they lament, "We yearned for happiness, we accumulated much wealth and property, we pursued every avenue of pleasure we could find. But though we have sought enjoyment here and there, still we have failed to achieve genuine peace of heart! We set out on an aimless, senseless journey! We expected happiness, yet we find ourselves drained, left only with vain illusions."

Why is it that so many reap such bitter disappointment as the fruit of all their endeavours? The reason is that they are ignorant of what constitutes real happiness. What people consider to be happiness is merely a feeling of pleasure born within their own minds. Unaware of the true nature of feeling, they delude themselves into thinking, "*I am* feeling this pleasure." They cling to their trifling pleasures and seek ever more pleasure, unaware that their very quest sets the stage for disappointment, misery, and despair.

Feelings of pleasure have no permanent core. They are ephemeral; they cannot be bent to satisfy our desires; we do not possess any mastery over them. When one pleasure fades away, at once people run in pursuit of fresh pleasure, seeking new pastures of enjoyment. Not even for a moment do they pause to reflect that their course of activity actually constitutes one mass of suffering. Neither are they aware that their greed for illusory pleasure leads to even greater suffering in the future. In this manner, while blindly wallowing in a mass of suffering, they become enslaved to craving, which in turn engenders only a further accumulation of misery. Thus the frightful wheel of existence rolls on without interruption, bringing still more suffering, never genuine happiness or peace.

The Buddha, who perfectly comprehended our existential plight, has clarified for us the real nature of both sorrow and happiness. He declares that conditioned existence, in its true nature, is fraught with suffering. Craving, rooted in ignorance of the true nature of existence, is the cause of suffering. Eradication of craving brings release from suffering and the attainment of true happiness. The means of achieving freedom from suffering lies in the cultivation of the Noble Eightfold Path, which cuts through all defilements anchored in craving and ignorance.

Each individual must personally realize true happiness through the eradication of the mind's defilements. As suffering is born within one's own mind, it must be overcome within one's own mind. None can impart freedom from suffering to another. To accomplish this aim one first has to understand suffering and its cause, and then to develop the path leading to release. Insight meditation, or *vipassanā-bhāvanā*, is the plan of action culminating in final liberation. Apart from the development of insight there is no other way to deliverance from suffering. The Pāli word *vipassanā* (insight) means "specialized and diversified vision" (*visesa-vividha-passanā*); it is the understanding of the real nature of phenomena through direct, immediate experience.[1] *Bhāvanā* (meditation) means "mental development." Hence *vipassanā-bhāvanā* means the *development of true insight into the nature of things as an experience in one's own mind.*

Several basic requirements have to be satisfied before one can pursue the practice of insight meditation with success. Let us briefly consider the most important of these.

For a beginner, it is desirable to practise meditation under the guidance of an experienced meditation master. Even though the student may be very learned in the Buddhist scriptures, as he is journeying along a strange path, many occasions may arise when he needs instruction and advice.[2] Hence the personal supervision of an accomplished master is recommended. If one cannot practise directly under the meditation master, in order to obtain the required guidance one should occasionally inform him of the progress of one's meditation by visiting him or even by correspondence.[3] If such guidance cannot be obtained from a qualified master, then one must arouse the necessary motivation to practise on one's own and seek guidance from reliable books; for during the period when the Buddha's Teaching still exists in the world it is our duty to obtain the maximum benefit from the fortunate human birth that has come our way.

Prior to commencing meditation proper, it is essential to achieve a satisfactory degree of seclusion by eliminating the physical and mental impediments (*paḷibodha*) that obstruct the unbroken progress of meditative development.[4] This does not imply that meditation cannot be practised merely because the impediments are present. Certain meditators practise amidst many impediments and achieve impressive results by utilizing their difficulties as a spur to effort. Yet even such meditators must overcome the main impediments, at least temporarily, during their periods of practice. On the other hand, the meditator who has found sufficient seclusion to develop the practice should be wary not to fall victim to indolence and complacency on account of that very freedom from external obstacles.

At the outset the meditator should become firmly established in the appropriate code of morality (*sīla*). The lay follower should observe the five, eight, or ten precepts of the laity; the novice and the fully ordained bhikkhu should adhere to their respective codes of monastic rules. Thereby they can achieve purity of conduct (*sīla-visuddhi*). Simultaneously, they should carefully develop those other principles crucial to the success of meditation: restraint of the six sense faculties (*indriyasaṁvara-sīla*)—eyes, ears, nose, tongue, body, and mind; the knowledge of the right measure in eating (*bhojane mattaññutā*); and the elimination of defilements through wakefulness (*jāgariyānuyoga*). As the influence of defilements becomes weakened through these measures, one becomes capable of continuing the meditation with success.

Before deciding on a major meditation subject, it may be of benefit to condition the mind for prolonged practice by meditating initially on the four recollections (also called the four basic or protective meditation subjects): the recollection of the virtues of the Buddha, the meditation on loving-kindness, attention to the impurity of the body, and mindfulness of death.[5] The meditation master should be watchful to see whether the practitioner has an innate aptitude to develop serenity (*samatha*) meditation.

At this point certain aptitudes and proclivities from previous lives may come to the fore. If the meditator finds that he can develop serenity meditation easily, he should continue deepening concentration through a congenial meditation subject. Thereby he should suppress the five hindrances[6] and try to attain jhāna, meditative absorption.[7] If he is successful in generating a jhāna, he should carefully safeguard it and attain mastery over it. This will enable the meditator to embark on insight meditation with that jhānic concentration as the basis. Alternatively, instead of turning to insight meditation immediately after gaining the first jhāna, he may first develop serenity meditation through the successive higher jhānas and turn to insight meditation only later.[8]

Those who find it difficult to develop serenity meditation to the level of absorption, or who have no suitable environment or time to suit its practice, may begin to develop insight meditation after achieving a basic degree of concentration through a general subject of meditation such as the four mentioned just above or mindfulness of breathing. This approach may also be taken by those who have an innate proclivity for insight meditation. By thus cultivating a subject of insight meditation, the hindrances will be abandoned through the "substitution of opposites" (*tadaṅga-pahāna*),[9] resulting in concentration (*samādhi*).[10]

This condition wherein the mind has become purified through the removal of the five hindrances, whether by means of the practice of serenity meditation or by insight meditation, is designated purification of mind (*cittavisuddhi*). It is on this foundation that true insight-wisdom unfolds.

The Three Stages of Insight

A short discourse by the Buddha, found in the Aṅguttara Nikāya, offers us a brief overview of the path of insight meditation. Here the Buddha describes the questions that a jhāna-attainer, devoid of insight-wisdom, might pose to one who has arrived at insight-wisdom, along with the answers that the insight meditator might give:

1. "Friend, how should formations be viewed?"[11]

   "Friend, formations should be viewed in such and such a way."

2. "How should formations be comprehended?"

   "Formations should be comprehended in such and such a way."

3. "How should formations be seen with insight?"

   "Formations should be seen with insight in such and such a way."[12]

Through this catechistic method, a threefold course of instruction is disclosed which corresponds to three stages in the process of insight meditation. These are the stages of: (i) viewing, (ii) comprehending, and (iii) gaining insight. Now let us briefly investigate how the path of insight can be defined on this basis.

(i) *The Stage of Viewing*

The meditator undertaking insight meditation first has to discern the ultimate constituents of actuality discoverable through the chosen subject of meditation. Let us take as an example a meditator who develops meditation on the four elements (*dhātuvavatthāna*). He begins by defining the parts of the body belonging to the earth element. He first directs attention to the earth element of the hair, which is manifest as its all-pervasive hardness. By intensifying his attention further, he comprehends the ultimate nature of the earth element in the hair, discriminating the solid or hard quality from the gross appearance of the hairs. He also comprehends, in a similar way, the ultimate nature of the water, fire, and wind elements in the hair. Proceeding thus with each bodily constituent, he defines the ultimate elements inherent in all the thirty-two parts of the body. He realizes that all these bodily parts, composed of the four elements, constitute matter (*rūpa*). The knowledge, or element of consciousness, that emerges with each of these as an object is mind (*nāma*). Thus the meditator confirms through direct cognition that matter is one type of reality and mind is another. This stage is known as the knowledge of the delimitation of mind and matter (*nāmarūpa-pariccheda-ñāṇa*). Along with this purified knowledge there also arises the purified vision that "in reality there is only mind and matter; there is no independent being, no substantial individual." Accordingly, this stage is also designated purification of view (*diṭṭhi-visuddhi*).

As the meditator expands his attention further, the conditions responsible for the generation of mental and material phenomena become clear. This is known as the knowledge regarding the discernment of conditions (*paccayapariggaha-ñāṇa*). At this stage, by realizing clearly how living beings exist as a series of causes and effects, the meditator eliminates all doubt regarding the existence of beings in the past, the present, and the future. This results in the next major stage of progress, purification by overcoming doubt (*kaṅkhāvitaraṇa-visuddhi*).

This is how the *stage of viewing* is accomplished. What basically happens here is that the meditator discerns the particular characteristics (*paccatta-lakkhaṇa*) of each of those conditioned phenomena pertaining to the meditation subject, and accordingly comes to realize that in the ultimate sense there is no being or individual but only a continuity of conditioned phenomena occurring in a causal chain. This stage is designated full understanding of the known (*ñāta-pariññā*).[13]

(ii) *The Stage of Comprehending*

Here the meditator examines the psycho-physical assemblage of phenomena continuing unbroken in a cause-effect series. Considering them from different angles and in certain fixed groups (*kalāpa*), he comes to realize that because they constantly undergo origination and dissolution, they are stamped through and through with the mark of impermanence (*anicca*). He also realizes that all such phenomena, being subject to distress and fearfulness on account of that impermanence, are permeated with suffering (*dukkha*). As there is no substantial essence in this impermanent and miserable psycho-physical process, no core that might be regarded as a self, he concludes that it is non-self (*anattā*). This initial grasp of the fact that all groups of formations taken up for examination are, without exception, marked by these three characteristics—impermanence, suffering, and selflessness—is called the knowledge of comprehension (*sammasana-ñāṇa*).

With the further maturation of the knowledge of comprehension, the meditator begins to see clearly how all formations on which he focuses, along with their causes and conditions, originate and dissolve right before his eyes. Accordingly, he ascertains that the three characteristics are invariably valid. This is the immature stage of the knowledge regarding the rise and fall of phenomena (*taruṇa-udayabbaya-ñāṇa*). At this point the corruptions of insight (*vipassan'upakkilesa*), such as the appearance of light, may become manifest.[14] The meditator realizes that to become deluded by these corruptions is to deviate from the path of meditative development and that the correct path is to abide by his chosen subject of meditation. This is the purification of knowledge and vision regarding the correct path and the wrong path (*maggāmaggañāṇa-dassana-visuddhi*). When he eradicates the corruptions of insight by clearly discriminating between the two paths, there dawns, quite powerfully, the mature knowledge regarding the rise and fall of phenomena (*balava-udayabbaya-ñāṇa*). This is the beginning of the purification by knowledge and vision of the way (*paṭipadāñāṇadassana-visuddhi*).

At this point the *stage of comprehension* (*sammasana*) becomes perfected. Here one is able to gain a decisive insight regarding the three common or general characteristics (*sāmañña-lakkhaṇa*) of all formations—namely, their impermanence, suffering, and selfless nature—which one penetrates with increasing clarity. This stage is therefore defined as that of full understanding by investigation (*tīraṇa-pariññā*).[15]

(iii) *The Stage of Gaining Insight*

This stage indicates how insight is practised on an intensified level by observing wisely, and in diverse ways, the operation of the three characteristics in all formations. The mature knowledge of the rise and fall of phenomena uncovers both the origination and the dissolution of formations. As this knowledge advances, at a certain point the meditator begins to see only the dissolution of phenomena and not their origination. This is the stage of knowledge of dissolution (*bhaṅga-ñāṇa*). Then, in sequence, one comes to acquire: the knowledge of the appearance of terror (*bhayat'upaṭṭhāna-ñāṇa*), which gives the meditator a definite conviction of the fearfulness in the incessant dissolution of formations; the knowledge of danger (*ādīnava-ñāṇa*), when one sees formations to be full of faults; and the knowledge of revulsion (*nibbidā-ñāṇa*), which makes one turn away from formations. Thereafter, one develops the knowledge of desire for deliverance (*muñcitu-kamyatā-ñāṇa*), prompting one to seek freedom from these formations, followed by the knowledge of reflection (*paṭisaṅkhā-ñāṇa*), which repeatedly reviews the three characteristics as a means for attaining freedom. This is followed by the knowledge of equanimity towards formations (*saṅkhār'upekkhā-ñāṇa*). When the knowledge of the three characteristics becomes sharper here, it leads to the knowledge of conformity (*anuloma-ñāṇa*), when the mind fixes on a single one of the three characteristics as its impetus for making the breakthrough to the Deathless. Thereafter, abandoning all formations as the object of knowledge, one transcends the "mundane lineage" and passes into "the lineage of the noble ones," as the knowledge of change-of-lineage (*gotrabhū-ñāṇa*) arises directly cognizing the peace of Nibbāna for the first time.

Subsequently, the meditator completes the realization of the Four Noble Truths by attaining the knowledge of the path of stream-entry (*sotāpattimagga-ñāṇa*). With this he totally eliminates, right down to their subtlest roots, the three fetters: the false view of personality (*sakkāya-diṭṭhi*), doubt (*vicikicchā*), and attachment to rites and rituals (*sīlabbata-parāmāsa*). Next, as the result of the supramundane path, he achieves the knowledge of fruition (*phala-ñāṇa*), which experiences the blissful peace of Nibbāna. Following fruition there arises reviewing knowledge (*paccavekkhaṇa-ñāṇa*), by which the meditator reviews the path, the fruit, and Nibbāna; he also reviews the defilements that have been eliminated and the defilements that remain.[16]

With the attainment of the knowledge of conformity, the purification of knowledge and vision pertaining to the way (*paṭipadāñāṇadassana-visuddhi*) is perfected. In the scheme of the seven purifications, the attainment of the knowledge of the path is designated the purification by knowledge and vision (*ñāṇadassana-visuddhi*).

The phase of practice ranging from the knowledge of dissolution to the knowledge of conformity can be regarded as the stage of gaining insight, which perfects full understanding by abandoning (*pahāna-pariññā*).[17] At this stage the abandoning of defilements through the "substitution of opposites" (*tadaṅga-pahāna*) takes precedence, each factor of insight serving to eliminate, temporarily, the particular defilement or cognitive distortion to which it is directly opposed.[18]

The foregoing account delineates the path of insight from a general viewpoint. Although this fundamental pattern is common, variations may occur in the experiences of individual meditators depending on their temperaments. For one meditator certain stages might be quite prominent, while other stages are not so prominent; certain stages might reach completion quickly, while others progress slowly. At times, for various reasons, one's attention may become broken, resulting in retrogression. Consequently one should respectfully follow the instructions given by the meditation master in regard to the unique experiences through which one may pass. Here we can provide only general guidelines.

As we expect to explain matters later on a more practical basis, the reader should bear in mind the general instructions so far presented.

...nsight in various ways. The ... to call attention to one classi- ... the progress of insight as a ... *...ssanā*).

...ns "seeing in different modes ... *...sanā* has been used in varying contexts. Thus the four foundations of mindfulness are called contemplations (e.g. *kāyānupassanā*, contemplation of the body); certain established insight knowledges are so described (e.g. *udayabbayānupassanā-ñāṇa*, knowledge of contemplation of rise and fall, and *bhaṅgānupassanā-ñāṇa*, knowledge of contemplation of dissolution).[20] In fact, every form of insight knowledge can be treated as a contemplation.

Practically speaking, both terms, *vipassanā* and *anupassanā*, are very similar in meaning, but in the present context *anupassanā* refers to special modes of attention contributing to the maturation of insight knowledge. These contemplations are not identical with the established insight knowledges; they are, rather, cognitive evaluations contributing to the emergence and development of those insight knowledges. At times certain contemplations may function in the role of the established insight knowledges, but often it may be necessary for several contemplations to function alternately for a particular insight knowledge to attain maturity. Conversely, the same contemplation may surface at different stages of insight development, thus providing support for several types of insight knowledge.

References to various contemplations of insight can be found scattered in the Buddha's discourses. Although the term *anupassanā* may not occur in all these contexts, the practices described evidently belong to that category.

A collection of eighteen contemplations is preserved in the *Paṭisambhidāmagga*, a treatise in the Khuddaka Nikāya of the

Sutta Piṭaka,[21] where we also find the fundamental pattern of the accepted sequence of insight knowledges. In many passages of this work insight is defined in relation to this series of contemplations, which the commentary describes as "the eighteen principal insights" (*aṭṭhārasa-mahāvipassanā*). Sometimes series of ten, nine, seven, or three of these contemplations are also mentioned.[22] Accordingly, commentarial and sub-commentarial works such as the *Visuddhimagga* have also occasionally given prominence to this group of eighteen.[23] One striking feature in this series of contemplations is that one defilement is eliminated by every contemplation developed, that is, eliminated through the substitution of opposites.

The first seven of these eighteen principal insights are presented as an independent group several times in the *Paṭisambhidāmagga*, which shows that they enjoy an elevated position among the other contemplations.[24] The commentaries and sub-commentaries, particularly the *Visuddhimagga*, introduce them under the name "the seven contemplations" (*sattānupassanā*), and on several occasions use them to analyse the progress of insight.[25] When considered from a practical point of view, the system based on this sevenfold group appears to be self-sufficient, and, as we shall see in the course of this work, insight can be analysed in its entirety through these contemplations.

The *Visuddhimagga* (XX,90) defines these seven as follows:

1. One who develops the contemplation of impermanence (*anicca*) abandons the perception of permanence.
2. One who develops the contemplation of suffering (*dukkha*) abandons the perception of pleasure.
3. One who develops the contemplation of non-self (*anattā*) abandons the perception of self.
4. One who develops the contemplation of revulsion (*nibbidā*) abandons delight.

5. One who develops the contemplation of dispassion (*virāga*) abandons passion.
6. One who develops the contemplation of cessation (*nirodha*) abandons origination.
7. One who develops the contemplation of relinquishment (*paṭinissagga*) abandons grasping.

These seven can be briefly explained as follows:

1. One who repeatedly contemplates the impermanence of formations (*aniccānupassanā*) relinquishes the wrong perception that formations are permanent (*niccasaññā*).
2. One who repeatedly contemplates the suffering (*dukkhānupassanā*) involved in formations relinquishes the wrong perception that formations are pleasurable (*sukhasaññā*).
3. One who repeatedly contemplates the selflessness of formations (*anattānupassanā*) relinquishes the wrong perception that formations have the nature of a self (*attasaññā*).
4. One who repeatedly contemplates the repulsiveness of formations (*nibbidānupassanā*) relinquishes delight (*nandi*), that is, the craving associated with joy tied up with formations.
5. One who repeatedly contemplates dispassion towards formations (*virāgānupassanā*) relinquishes passion (*rāga*), that is, attachment to formations.
6. One who repeatedly contemplates the cessation of formations (*nirodhānupassanā*) relinquishes origination (*samudaya*), that is, the desire that causes formations to continue emerging again and again.
7. One who repeatedly develops the contemplation of relinquishment (*paṭinissaggānupassanā*) abandons grasping (*ādāna*), that is, the seizing of formations.

Here, the term *bhāvento* means "one who develops." This term has a wide range of meanings and, in its broadest implications, extends to the entire path of insight meditation. Briefly stated, it points to the development of the contemplation leading to the emergence of the thirty-seven constituents of enlightenment.

From the next chapter onwards the seven contemplations will be described individually in sequence. The discussion will deal with the nature of each contemplation, the manner of their emergence in insight meditation, their functional variations at different stages of the insight process, their relations with different insight knowledges, how the respective defilements are eliminated by each contemplation, and other important matters. Attempts will be made to keep the discussion as practical as possible. Due attention will also be paid to similarities and contrasts among the contemplations as well as to pertinent allusions made to them in the canonical texts and commentaries. Once all the contemplations have been scrutinized individually, a synoptic analysis will be presented.

1

Contemplation of Impermanence (*Aniccānupassanā*)

> One who develops the contemplation of impermanence abandons the perception of permanence.
>
> (*Aniccānupassanaṁ bhāvento niccasaññaṁ pajahati.*)

The Characteristic of Impermanence

Let us begin by examining the meaning of the term "impermanence" (*aniccatā*). The term "impermanence," or the characteristic of impermanence, signifies the nature of not being permanent, of not being everlasting, of originating and dissolving, of wasting away, decaying, and undergoing transformation, etc. Arising is the beginning of impermanence; decay is its middle point; dissolution is its end.[1] This characteristic of impermanence is common to all the formations comprised in the five aggregates that make up our empirical personality: material form, feeling, perception, mental formations (the volitional factors), and consciousness. These five aggregates are designated "formations" (*saṅkhārā*) because they originate from a combination of conditions and disappear with the transformation of those conditions. Here it is important to distinguish between *a thing that is impermanent* and *the characteristic of impermanence*. Formations—the five aggregates themselves—are impermanent; they are the things that are impermanent. Their inherent nature of not remaining permanently, of undergoing transformation, is the characteristic of impermanence.

Formations themselves demonstrate this impermanence. A wise person with a developed mind will be able to discern the impermanence of formations hidden beneath the most common events of ordinary life. A flower bud appears at the end of a branch and gradually blossoms forth into a beautiful, fragrant flower; then after it has matured, it withers away, falls to the ground, and decomposes. Don't we constantly encounter profound revelations of impermanence even in the simplest incidents of daily life?

If we examine the matter intelligently, we will notice how impermanence is at work not only in the external world but also within ourselves—in our own five aggregates. How many transformations have you undergone from the time you first appeared in the uterus as an almost indiscernible tiny foetus? Not only do we change from year to year and from day to day, but we change at every moment. The action you performed a moment ago has now ended. The thought that came to your mind an instant earlier is now no more. This constant passing away of whatever rises shows that impermanence is an intrinsic fact of life, one which cannot be separated from the five aggregates that make up your very being.[2]

The ignorant worldling who fails to grasp this truth regards his own personal five aggregates as well as external objects as permanent. Accordingly, all his mental, verbal, and physical actions will be based on erroneous assumptions. His ignorance of the true situation, and the unwholesome deeds he performs on account of that ignorance, make him a victim of suffering, anxiety, and stress. Bound to the vicious cycle of rebirths (*saṁsāra*), he cannot realize true happiness and peace.

Even though formations shout out in every direction, "We are impermanent," we still find it difficult to discard the perception of permanence, which, through prolonged habit over countless lives, is embedded so deeply in our minds. No matter how often we hear about impermanence, read about impermanence, think about impermanence, that alone is not capable of replacing our habitual perception of permanence with the direct perception of impermanence in its stark reality.

Special effort is required to alter our modes of perception: first we have to make the mind stable, then we have to see for ourselves how formations are impermanent, how they continually arise and break apart. Such a perception can only be generated by the actual practice of insight meditation.[3]

Contemplation or *anupassanā* refers to the continuously repeated occupation of one's powers of observation with one's chosen object of meditation as one engages in the practice of insight meditation. This observation or "seeing" involves the application of mindfulness and wisdom. It is also described as the application of mindfulness and full awareness (*sati-sampajañña*) and as wise attention (*yoniso manasikāra*). Repeated inspection, with insight knowledge, of the characteristic of impermanence in regard to the five impermanent aggregates is what is called the contemplation of impermanence (*aniccānupassanā*). This replaces the perception of permanence with the direct perception of impermanence.[4]

Uncovering the Mark of Impermanence

There is a dignified plan of action by following which the contemplation of impermanence can be successfully accomplished. This plan unfolds step by step from the most basic preliminaries of insight meditation to the stage called the full understanding of the known (*ñāta-pariññā*). At the outset, after becoming established on a foundation of purified morality, the meditator suppresses the five hindrances and achieves concentration. Thereafter, with a well concentrated mind, he directly perceives the psycho-physical formations through their individual or particular characteristics (*paccatta-lakkhaṇa*). He further discerns their causes and conditions, and through this meditational knowledge comes to realize that the entire compound of the five aggregates is merely a natural continuity of phenomena bound together as causes and effects. With the further refinement of mindfulness and awareness, the meditator also realizes that in each material form, hitherto regarded as a single entity, there are actually many constituents revealing themselves one after another. He also sees that even the mental states apprehending these sense objects are subject to continuous disintegration. Here he comprehends the changing nature of these psycho-physical entities (*nāma-rūpadhamma*). Through this knowledge he understands how origination and dissolution come about, thereby realizing the characteristic of impermanence.

Let us take an example for further clarification. A meditator practising mindfulness of breathing with a concentrated mind directs his attention to the in-breath and the out-breath coming into contact either with the upper lip or the tip of the nose.[5] Initially he would see any given in-breath or out-breath as a single uniform entity. But later, as his mindfulness and concentration improve, his attention becomes so precise that he can discern the beginning, the middle, and the end phases within any single breath, whether inward or outward.[6] At this point the intermediate phases of each inhalation and exhalation become quite obvious to him. Gradually, he comes to understand that within each of these stages there are further divisions in a sequential process. Simultaneously, he also sees their appearance and disappearance and eventually it becomes clear to him that not only the observed phenomenon but even the contemplating mind is subject to a process of origination and dissolution. In this manner the characteristic of impermanence becomes manifest.

The characteristic of impermanence cannot be easily observed because it is obscured by the characteristic of continuity. Through its conceptual activity the mind grasps the continuity of events as a compact mass, conceiving the sequential psycho-physical process as a single whole.[7] For this reason one sees the psycho-physical phenomena as existing permanently and not as a sequential process subject to origination and dissolution. It is only by attending to the phenomena with extremely keen attention, empowered by continuous practice, that one can actually perceive the discrete origination and dissolution of the particular psycho-physical phenomena normally concealed by the notion of continuity. Through the power of directed attention one can dispel the perception of the process as a compact mass and thereby perceive the discrete phenomena in their precise particularity. With the maturation of the discernment of conditions (*paccaya-pariggaha*)—that is, the observation of the conditions for the psycho-physical phenomena—those psycho-physical phenomena that become the objects of one's mind should be carefully contemplated in relation to their beginning, middle, and end.[8] Doing so will make manifest the rise and fall of each of these phenomena and will thereby dissolve the concept of the continuity of events as a compact mass. This will usher in the realization of the characteristic of impermanence.[9]

It would also be beneficial to the understanding of impermanence to consider the following four factors that help to expose the impermanence involved in all formations:

1. Everything that exists is marked by origination and dissolution.
2. Nothing remains without changing.
3. All phenomena are momentary or temporary.
4. There is no permanency anywhere.[10]

In insight meditation it is advisable to allow the characteristic of impermanence to surface naturally. For this to occur, as a prerequisite the knowledge regarding the discernment of conditions must first be matured.[11] This ushers in the purification by overcoming doubt (*kaṅkhāvitaraṇa-visuddhi*), in the trail of which the concept of "I" is eclipsed in the meditator's mind. The meditator comes to realize that personal existence is only a cause-effect process of phenomena and that there exists no permanent core that can be grasped as a truly existent "I" either inside or outside his own five aggregates. Therefore, when the meditational knowledge arises discerning the five aggregates as impermanent, the meditator will be able to accept the impermanence of formations with equanimity, free from trepidation. If the characteristic of impermanence should appear while he still retains the sense of "I"—due to the incompleteness of his knowledge regarding the discernment of conditions—he might become frightened at the loss of his sense of ego and might even be tempted to abandon meditation altogether.

Venerable Channa was an obstinate monk who had to be disciplined by the Sangha with the highest punishment after the passing away of the Buddha. The other monks had agreed that they would completely ignore him unless he changed his ways. He had been practising insight meditation on impermanence and non-self without having developed the knowledge regarding the discernment of conditions. As a consequence he became frightened. He felt as if his "self" were falling into an abyss and thought, "What has happened to my 'self'? Oh, I am going to be annihilated!" Thus fear overcame him.[12] Similarly, when the Buddha first expounded the Four Noble Truths, the deities of long life became thoroughly frightened on learning of their impermanent state, as deer become frightened on hearing the lion's roar.[13] Hence, at the very beginning of one's meditative training it is not advisable to focus attention on the characteristic of impermanence.

The *contemplation of impermanence* is the repeated observation of the impermanence of the five aggregates comprehended through the meditation itself. This contemplation should be allowed to progress until the perception of impermanence becomes well established in one's mind. Very often, in the initial stages of the contemplation of impermanence, one may distinctly observe the breaking up in groups of the materiality connected with the primary meditation subject (e.g. the in-and-out breathing or the movement of the abdomen). Subsequently, the impermanence of the mental factors will also become clear, leading to a general conviction that the complex of the five aggregates is impermanent in its entirety. Based on this conviction one contemplates the aggregates external to one's own personal aggregates—that is, the aggregates of other persons and of external nature—as being impermanent too. By inference from the impermanence that is directly visible, one concludes that all formations in the past were impermanent and that all formations in the future will likewise be impermanent. Confirming the impermanence of the psycho-physical phenomena in this concise manner, by classifying them into such various groups, adds strength to the knowledge of comprehension (*sammasana-ñāṇa*).[14]

As mindfulness and awareness become sharper, the meditator clearly discerns the continuous origination and dissolution of any single object that comes under his observation right in the present moment. This insight yields an even stronger conviction of the characteristic of impermanence. The causative factors behind the origination and dissolution of each aggregate also become manifest. This is the "tender" stage of the knowledge regarding the rise and fall of phenomena.[15] If one is misled by the corruptions of insight meditation (*vipassan'upakkilesa*) arising at this stage and indulges in the enjoyment of them, the contemplation on impermanence will become feeble and will eventually collapse. The deft meditator applies the perception of impermanence to all the impediments that arise in the course of contemplation and thereby succeeds in clearing this hurdle. Thereafter, he will arrive at a vividly clear vision of the characteristic of impermanence and this will pave the way for the mature knowledge regarding the rise and fall of phenomena.

As the meditator progresses further in the contemplation of impermanence, at a certain point he transcends the concern with the origination of phenomena and takes dissolution alone as the object of attention. The knowledge of the contemplation of dissolution (*bhaṅgānupassanā-ñāṇa*) resulting from this is a power-packed product of the contemplation of impermanence. Following this knowledge, the contemplation of impermanence surfaces in diverse forms and becomes immensely helpful to the progress of the series of insight knowledges. When insight meditation reaches its consummation, it is possible the contemplation of impermanence may function as a door to liberation (*vimokkha-mukha*), directing the meditator towards the experience of Nibbāna by way of the signless liberation (*animitta-vimokkha*).[16] Thus we find that the contemplation of impermanence is a major contemplation covering the entire gamut of the path of insight. For this reason, in our discussion of the other contemplations in the following chapters, the contemplation of impermanence will frequently reappear in different forms.

Development and Abandoning

The term "one who develops" (*bhāvento*), mentioned in the opening stanza of our discussion, indicates the plan of action conducive to the development of contemplation. As much has already been stated in this context, we here present only four main common factors that help in the realization of all the contemplations. These are:

1. Maintaining in balance the twin faculties of confidence and wisdom on the one hand, and effort and concentration on the other, as they are generated in the mind in the pursuit of meditation.
2. An equalized maturation of all the faculties—confidence, wisdom, effort, concentration, and mindfulness, and their being directed to a single purpose.
3. Maintenance of effort to the standard required for the purpose of meditation—neither too strained nor too loose.
4. Reinforcement by constant practice.[17]

Many positive results may be obtained from the application of attention in meditation, results that are lofty and serene as well. If one wants to achieve these lofty and serene results, one has to apply oneself with a mind consistently strong and well charged with determination.

The term "abandons" (*pajahati*) implies the advantages accruing from the development of contemplation. This is the disappearance of the corresponding defilements by way of "the substitution of opposites."[18] Defilements are eliminated in insight meditation somewhat in the way darkness disappears with the rising of the sun: the one drives away the other through its opposite nature without permanently eradicating it. Therefore, when the power of contemplation weakens, these defilements may surface again, just as the darkness returns when the sun sets. But if one can generate the wisdom of the supramundane path by developing the insight knowledges to perfection, those defilements that disappear with the realization of each path-knowledge are completely cut off and will never arise again.

The specific defilement eliminated through contemplation of impermanence is the perception of permanence, which is the wrong notion that "formations are permanent and everlasting." This distortion of perception (*saññā-vipallāsa*), which results from ignorance of the real nature of formations, gathers momentum through repeated occurrence and issues in a distortion of consciousness (*citta-vipallāsa*). This in turn, through further maturation, engenders a distortion of views (*diṭṭhi-vipallāsa*).[19] Eventually this wrong conviction that "formations are permanent" becomes so strongly confirmed in the mind that its elimination is a Herculean task.

How many times must this concept of permanence have arisen in our minds throughout this beginningless cycle of rebirths! And as a result, how deeply embedded must the distorted view of permanence have become in our minds! Therefore, although we are ever and again confronted with the impermanence of formations, we consistently ignore these revelations of truth and let ourselves indulge in vain thoughts of acquisition and enjoyment, thereby reinforcing the dominance of the wrong perception of permanence over our minds. Thus, even though we hear and see the dictum "all formations are impermanent" on all sides, we become deeply grieved at the death of someone very close to us. While we are offered the excellent opportunity of realizing this great truth, the concept of permanence rules our minds so imperiously that we find it almost impossible to fix our attention on the mark of impermanence. In a short time, as our sorrow diminishes, we settle back comfortably into our accustomed lifestyle once again, with our view of permanence reconfirmed.

The case is quite different with the diligent meditator who develops the contemplation of impermanence with a concentrated mind. With the meditator, the concept of permanence cannot get even a foothold in his thoughts, for he realizes the impermanent nature of formations through direct perception. Thus there is no chance for any distortion of mind or any distortion of views to arise in him in regard to the idea of permanence. Further, he recognizes that the very notion of permanence—whether as a perception, a thought, or a view—which had previously been rooted so deeply in the mind, has begun to wear away.

As the contemplation of impermanence becomes strengthened through repeated development, the perception of permanence subsides completely and the perception of impermanence becomes uppermost in the mind. The meditator realizes that all the formations of the three worlds inclusive of his own five aggregates are constantly changing and breaking up. Thus, as he goes on repeatedly developing the contemplation of impermanence in relation to the impermanent group of five aggregates, he abandons the wrong notion, thought, and view that "the five aggregates are permanent and everlasting."

* * *

"O monks, a monk who clearly sees six benefits should set up without limits the perception of impermanence in relation to all formations. These six are:

1. 'All formations will appear to me as unstable.'
2. 'My mind will not take delight in all the three worlds (sensuous, fine-material, and immaterial).'
3. 'My mind will emerge from all the three worlds.'
4. 'My mind will be oriented towards Nibbāna.'
5. 'The fetters will be abandoned by me.'
6. 'I will be endowed with supreme recluseship.'"[20]

2

Contemplation of Suffering (*Dukkhānupassanā*)

> One who develops the contemplation of suffering abandons the perception of pleasure.
>
> (*Dukkhānupassanaṁ bhāvento sukhasaññaṁ pajahati.*)

The Characteristic of Suffering

In a debate with the disputant Saccaka the Buddha used the following line of argument to convince him that the five aggregates involve suffering:

> "Aggivessana, what do you think, are material form, feeling, perception, mental formations, and consciousness permanent or impermanent?"
> "Venerable Gotama, they are impermanent."
> "If a thing is impermanent, is it pleasurable or painful?"
> "Venerable Gotama, it is painful."[1]

Many other discourses of the Master are cast in the same mould. Accordingly, the five aggregates themselves, precisely because they are impermanent, are necessarily suffering as well. The nature of suffering inherent in the five aggregates is referred to as the characteristic of suffering (*dukkhalakkhaṇa*). This characteristic of suffering is nothing but the oppression, the suppression, the obstruction, and the fearfulness brought about by the continuous origination and dissolution of the aggregates.[2]

The suffering inherent in the five aggregates is a daily experience of ours in very much the same way as their impermanence is. Yet conviction regarding this truth eludes us because we fail to recognize this suffering as suffering. If we remain immobile for some time in the same posture, or stand in the sweltering sun, or get even a simple ailment like a headache or a toothache, we experience physical pains and aches. Ordinarily, we promptly dismiss such painful feelings as evanescent and adventitious, but by doing so we fail to see that every such experience of physical pain is an unmistakable reminder of the reality of the ever-present suffering grounded in the impermanent nature of material form. How many occasions are there in our day-to-day life when physical suffering is brought into focus?

Sorrow springs up when we are separated from loved ones and from cherished objects. We become angry, jealous, and anxious when the objects of our attention are unwelcome. Grief, distress, and aversion overcome us when our expectations are disappointed. So often in the course of our lives do we experience distress because of the impermanent nature of things! This bodily pain and psychological distress are together designated "intrinsic suffering" (*dukkha-dukkha*); they are so called because they are painful both by designation and by nature.[3]

After waking up in the morning you wash your face, brush your teeth, and perhaps shave. Although you engage in these activities day in and day out as routine habits, have you even once given thought to how troublesome they really are? If you analyse the situation realistically you will recognize that the entire process is just a heap of suffering. It would be consoling if you could keep the cleansed condition of the body after washing once. But just imagine the amount of trouble one has to undergo in repeating the process two or three times a day for a whole lifetime! Isn't our life full of such repetitive, cumbersome activities resulting from the continuous alteration of formations? When one meets some difficulty in breathing, as when one has a blocked nose or bronchitis, one can see that even continuous inhalation and exhalation involve suffering. Can we estimate the extent of suffering we experience during our lifetime in our endeavour to obtain and safeguard the requisites for the maintenance of life? Owing to the rise and fall of the formations, their care and maintenance involves much suffering, which is accordingly designated "suffering due to formations" (*saṅkhāra-dukkha*).

While living in the midst of such a mass of affliction we remain bogged down in it because we live in constant hope of the pleasurable feelings we occasionally enjoy. We feel delighted when our eyes meet a pleasant sight, when our ears hear a sweet voice, when our nose catches a pleasing smell, when our tongue encounters something tasty, when our body feels a pleasant touch, and when our mind conceives of a delightful object of thought.[4] Yet these pleasant experiences do not remain permanently. They vanish along with the pleasurable objects from which they arise. This loss itself is suffering. As our wish for those delightful experiences to persist becomes frustrated, suffering arises. This aspect of suffering is designated "suffering due to change" (*vipariṇāma-dukkha*).[5] As the happiness wished for is soon lost, we are impelled to undergo further suffering in an attempt to regain more and more of that happiness.

Life, or the continuity of the five aggregates, which we assiduously grasp as "pleasure," is in reality a constant mass of suffering. The bliss obtained in the heavenly realms and the Brahma-worlds is only a temporary, partial mitigation of this affliction, not a genuine attainment of happiness. Moreover, it is impossible for anyone to stay in the heavens or the Brahma-worlds forever. Whatever be the form of becoming into which one is born, so long as one holds on to one's inheritance of formations one cannot escape suffering, for suffering is inherent in all formations.

Uncovering the Mark of Suffering

To realize the universality of suffering, one has to develop the contemplation of suffering, which is the repeated wise observation, with deep concentration, of the characteristic of suffering inherent in the five painful aggregates. Seeing suffering in its true perspective thus stabilizes the perception of suffering (i.e. the notion that "formations are nothing but a heap of suffering") well in one's mind.[6]

The main factor that obscures the characteristic of suffering from our minds is the habit of changing the postures. This habit, precisely because it is so commonplace, invites our special attention. There are four major postures: sitting, standing, walking, and lying down. We spend every minute of the day in one or another of these postures; we engage in every activity in one or another of these postures. Our very lives are intimately connected with them. A notion that "the postures bring comfort to us" has become implanted in our minds. Thus if we feel uncomfortable in one posture, we promptly change to another for the sake of immediate relief. We fail to see that the nature of suffering is inherent in every posture. In order to camouflage from ourselves this oppression constantly being generated by the rise and fall of phenomena, we hide inside a cocoon of comfort by changing our posture. Just reflect on how casually we readjust our posture in order to assuage the physical and mental stress impinging on us so poignantly throughout our waking life. Thus we should comprehend how the suffering inherent in the five aggregates becomes eclipsed through the spontaneous, unreflecting manipulation of the postures.

The meditator must grasp this condition well; one should reflect on the fact that each posture is a receptacle of suffering. One must come to know that we resort to a change of posture, not for the sake of pleasure, but because it is unavoidable in the course of maintaining a physical body. Since this is so, when one practises insight meditation one must be mindful of the suffering inherent in the postures. When it is necessary to change the posture, one should do so with total mindfulness of the change, aware why the change is being made. If we can act with this understanding, we won't be deluded by the assumption that suffering ceases with a change of posture, and thereby we will be disposed to realize the characteristic of suffering. Therefore, when the rise and fall of formations become evident, the meditator, while remaining totally attentive to the resulting stress, should not change the posture even slightly to avoid the stress. Then he will be able to discern the mark of suffering.[7]

It is pertinent to attend to the following four factors that also help to uncover the characteristic of suffering:

1. Strain and torment are recurrently experienced through the threefold suffering: intrinsic suffering, suffering due to formations, and suffering due to change.[8]
2. Unbearable stress results from this.
3. The five aggregates are the basis of this threefold suffering and for all the suffering of saṁsāra, the beginningless journey through countless lives.
4. Formations are devoid of any real pleasure.[9]

From the beginning of the meditation until he achieves tranquillity (*passaddhi,* i.e. physical and mental buoyancy) through the chosen object of meditation, the meditator will experience physical pains of diverse types.[10] At times he will encounter mental strain as well. This alone, however, will not enable him to penetrate the characteristic of suffering, for he has not yet properly penetrated the characteristic of impermanence.

The maturation of tranquillity brings about bliss (*sukha*), which in turn results in concentration,[11] and this is the condition that enables one to reach the discernment of mentality-materiality (*nāmarūpa-pariggaha*) and the discernment of the conditionality of all phenomena (*paccaya-pariggaha*).

Next, observing how the psycho-physical phenomena that appear in a cause-effect series perish in groups, one summarily realizes the characteristic of impermanence. By being mindful and aware of the oppressive, frightful nature of impermanent phenomena, one realizes the characteristic of suffering in a general way. Repeated application of mindfulness and awareness to the characteristic of suffering thus realized is designated the "contemplation of suffering" (*dukkhānupassanā*).

At this initial stage one can establish the characteristic of suffering on the basis of the impermanence of the aggregates by allocating the five aggregates to eleven groupings—past, present, or future, internal or external, gross or subtle, inferior or superior, far or near (see Chap. 1, n.14). The contemplation of suffering thus performed is helpful in stabilizing the knowledge of comprehension (*sammasana-ñāṇa*). Once this comprehension through meditation on groups reaches maturity, impermanence will become clearly manifest in every immediately known sense object. It then becomes easier to understand the characteristic of suffering. At this stage the knowledge of rise and fall (*udayabbaya-ñāṇa*) will begin to function, though if one becomes deluded by the corruptions of insight (*vipassan'upakkilesa*) contemplation of suffering will be weakened.

As the contemplation of impermanence grows stronger the knowledge of dissolution (*bhaṅga-ñāṇa*) arises. This knowledge makes abundantly clear the frightful nature of all formations on account of their incessant dissolution and thereby sharpens the contemplation of suffering. This contemplation gives rise in turn to the knowledge of appearance as terror (*bhayat'upaṭṭhāna-ñāṇa*). With further development of the contemplation of suffering, one discerns quite clearly the inherent defects of mentality-materiality and thus attains the knowledge of danger (*ādīnava-ñāṇa*). This is followed by the knowledge of revulsion (*nibbidā-ñāṇa*), which generates revulsion towards the five aggregates. This knowledge turns out to be a significant juncture in the progress of insight meditation, for revulsion is the experience that motivates the meditator to strive earnestly for the realization of Nibbāna.

Even in the subsequent stages of meditation the contemplation of suffering will operate in a variety of forms, thereby further strengthening the series of insight knowledges. If the contemplation of suffering takes precedence at the stage of the knowledge of conformity (*anuloma-ñāṇa*), it could even be an opening towards Nibbāna by way of the door of desireless liberation (*appaṇihita-vimokkhamukha*—see Chap. 1, n.16).

In this manner the contemplation of suffering, in unison with that of impermanence, plays an essential role in the successful completion of insight meditation. We will be discussing its different aspects in later chapters.

Development and Abandoning

In order to investigate a few ideas implied by the term *bhāvento* ("one who develops"), occurring in the epigram of this chapter, let us consider the following words of the Buddha:

> "Here, monks, a certain person lives contemplating the suffering involved in all formations, perceiving and experiencing it at all times without a break, without a lapse, without mixing his contemplation with any other thought; he mentally confirms it and immerses himself in it with the wisdom of insight."[12]

This passage delineates a programme of action commonly applicable to the development of all the contemplations. It may be summarized as follows:

1. One should develop contemplation at all times without a break.
2. The thought following any thought of contemplation should also be one of contemplation, in keeping with the preceding one; that is, one should generate thoughts of contemplation only, without a lapse.

3. One should not generate thoughts other than those of contemplation.
4. One should confirm in one's own mind the object of contemplation.
5. One should immerse oneself in the contemplation with wisdom.

These meditational skills can be regarded as a graded series of steps leading progressively from one to the next. The discourse quoted unveils a highly elevated standard in the development of contemplation. This type of practice will provide a foundation for attaining the roads to power (*iddhipāda*), which means that the meditator's efforts would be doubly successful.[13] This is confirmed by the fact that this discourse contains seven methods by which an insight meditator can attain either arahantship or the stage of non-returner (*anāgāmitā*) in this very life.

By developing the contemplation of suffering the perception of pleasure disappears. The perception of pleasure is the misconception or mistaken notion that the five aggregates are a source of pleasure. Although it originates merely as a distortion of perception (*saññāvipallāsa*), one should understand how, through repeated confirmation, this misconception can gather momentum and develop into a distortion of consciousness (*cittavipallāsa*) and a distortion of view (*diṭṭhivipallāsa*).[14] Observe for a while how deep-rooted in our minds is the notion that our senses and their objects—the eye and the forms it sees, the ear and the sounds it hears, the nose and the odours it smells, the tongue and the tastes it experiences, the body and the sensations it feels, the mind and its objects of thought—are all sources of pleasure for us. Although we become victims of various illnesses and related sufferings such as stress, loss, rebuke, disappointment, etc., thousands of times—nay, innumerable times—does the thought ever occur to us even momentarily that "these five aggregates are of the nature of suffering"? Deluded by the grievously mistaken view that "suffering and misfortune are adventitious; this world, this life is essentially pleasurable," we camouflage even the most acute form of suffering with the hope of some prospective pleasure. It is owing to the intensity of our perception of pleasure that we torment ourselves searching for permanent happiness in this world of formations, as a thirsty man runs in hot pursuit of a water-mirage.

When the meditator realizes, through the contemplation of suffering, how widespread is the oppressive and frightful nature of formations due to their incessant origination and cessation, and when he reflects how this same law holds sway over all the three worlds, he discovers that there is not even an iota of happiness obtainable from them. Consequently, he abandons the perception of pleasure in the five aggregates—a perception that had become uppermost in his mind throughout beginningless saṁsāra. He replaces this deluded perception with the true perception of suffering, the recognition that "the five aggregates are certainly of the nature of suffering."

In this manner, by repeatedly contemplating the nature of suffering resulting from the oppression of change inherent in the five aggregates, one who develops the contemplation of suffering abandons the perception, the thought, and the view that the five aggregates are pleasurable. Instead, he learns to see them as merely a mass of suffering.

* * *

> "O monks, when a monk sees six benefits, it should be enough for him to establish the perception of suffering towards all formations without exception. What six?
>
> 1. 'Towards all formations a perception of revulsion will be present in me, as towards a murderer with raised sword.'
> 2. 'My mind will emerge from all the three worlds.'

3. 'I shall be a seer of serenity in Nibbāna.'
4. 'The underlying tendencies (*anusaya*) will be extirpated by me.'
5. 'I shall be one who does his duty (as regards the four paths).'
6. 'I shall have waited upon the Teacher with loving ministration.'"[15]

3

Contemplation of Non-self

(*Anattānupassanā*)

> One who develops the contemplation of non-self abandons the perception of self.
>
> (*Anattānupassanaṁ bhāvento attasaññaṁ pajahati.*)

The Characteristic of Non-self

The term "non-self" (*anattā*) signifies the absence of an everlasting substance identifiable as a self, a being, a person, or some entity under one's control.[1] For purposes of communication we have to use terms such as "self," "being," or "person," etc., but all such terms of personal reference are solely conventional and do not denote anything existing independently of the five aggregates. Despite this hard fact, on account of ignorance many subtle thinkers from time immemorial have elaborated the spontaneous perception of self into the fixed view that a self really exists; that we are substantial beings; that at the core of every person there is an independent spiritual essence or soul. The Buddha's teaching runs "against the grain" of all these religious and philosophical speculations about a self precisely in its teaching of selflessness.

At the time the Buddha appeared in India most thinkers agreed that beings have a permanent self, though they sharply disagreed about the nature of that self. Some believed the self is infinite, others that it is finite; some identified it with perception, some with intelligence, some with bliss. The great majority said the self was spirit and would exist eternally, but an outspoken minority said the self was material and perished at death. All these views of self arose because they failed to penetrate the purely functional nature of the five aggregates. In such an age the Buddha, through his supreme knowledge of reality, declared that a real self does not exist anywhere in any way. Thereby, with his doctrine of non-self, he triggered off a major revolution in human thought.[2] By analysing beings in diverse ways into aggregates, elements, and sense spheres (*khandha-dhātu-āyatana*), he demonstrated that no entity can ever be taken as a self.[3] He further proved that because these formations occur as processes in a cause-effect relationship, they are not subject to control by a self.[4] He clearly demonstrated that in the face of the universal laws of impermanence and suffering, the very concept of a self collapses.[5]

In the Yavakalāpi Sutta of the Saṁyutta Nikāya the Buddha provides a trenchant account of how the perception of self becomes settled in the human mind.[6] He begins the discourse with a parable: Once upon a time the gods had defeated the *asuras* (titans) in battle. They bound the *asura* chief Vepacitti by a fivefold celestial bond and brought him into the presence of Sakka, king of the gods. Whenever the thought occurred to Vepacitti, "The gods are righteous and the *asuras* unrighteous; now I shall enter the city of the gods here itself," his bonds loosened and he could enjoy the five kinds of celestial sense pleasures. If he thought, "The *asuras* are righteous and the gods unrighteous; now I shall enter the city of the *asuras* here itself," the celestial sense pleasures disappeared and he found himself again bound by the fivefold bond.

Referring to this subtle celestial bondage wherein becoming bound or unbound depends on the very thoughts of the victim, the Buddha declares:

> "O monks, see how subtle the bondage of Vepacitti is; but the bondage of Māra the Evil One is even subtler. One who imagines is bound by the Evil One.[7] One who does not imagine is freed from the Evil One. 'I am' is an imag-

ining (*maññita*); 'I am this' is an imagining; 'I shall be' is an imagining; 'I shall not be' is an imagining; 'I shall possess material form' is an imagining; 'I shall be formless' is an imagining; 'I shall be conscious' is an imagining; 'I shall be unconscious' is an imagining; 'I shall be neither conscious nor unconscious' is an imagining. This imagining, monks, is a disease, a boil, a dart.

"Therefore, monks, you should train yourselves thus: 'Let us abide with our minds free from imaginings': that is how you should train yourselves, monks. 'I am' is an agitation (*iñjita*) ... 'I am' is a palpitation (*phandita*) ... 'I am' is a conceptual proliferation (*papañcita*) ... 'I am' is a conceit (*mānagata*)."

In order to understand this discourse well, let us inquire how this "imagining" takes place. Potent defilements lie dormant as underlying tendencies (*anusaya*) in the mundane consciousness of all unenlightened beings.[8] These include ignorance (*avijjā*), not knowing the truth; craving (*taṇhā*), attachment, desire, enjoyment, possessiveness; conceit (*māna*), application of the "I"-concept as the dominant standard of judgement; and view (*diṭṭhi*), adherence to a distorted opinion as truth. Unless one is mindful and thoroughly attentive when cognizing objects through the six sense faculties—the eye, ear, nose, tongue, body, and mind—these defilements will surface and become activated.[9]

Visual consciousness arises because of the eye and visible forms; the "coming together" of these three things—eye, forms, and consciousness—is contact; because of contact there arises feeling; whatever is felt is perceived. As in the case of the eye, this same process operates in relation to the other sense faculties as well.[10] Owing to ignorance one fails to comprehend this very rapid process. Hence the person with an undeveloped mind will exercise this perception in a perverted manner in keeping with deeply ingrained habit. Although the formations are in reality impermanent, foul, suffering, and non-self, we perceive them to be permanent, beautiful, a source of happiness, and self, and thereby we kindle the defilements of craving, conceit, and view. Consequently, the real nature of phenomena remains concealed beneath the false appearances that we erroneously ascribe to them. This error leads to the fabrication of mistaken notions, theories, and suppositions. The Buddha refers to this fabricating activity as "imagination" (*maññanā*) and to its products as "imaginings" (*maññita*).[11]

The Threefold Imagining

The above discourse helps us to identify three main stages in the unfolding of "imagination," culminating in a full-fledged view of a self. Let us now see how the process of imagining develops.

(i) *The imagining "I am" (asmi)*

Through the enjoyment of the feeling generated in relation to any of the six sense objects, the imaginative activity of craving (*taṇhā-maññanā*) comes into play based on the perverted perception. Governed by this imaginative activity, and again based on the perverted perception, the imaginative activity of conceit (*māna-maññanā*) starts, which leads to the conceiving of the sense object in terms of either "I" or "mine," or "he/she," or "his/hers." If this conceiving refers to other people, a further evaluation of them may occur by which they are ranked as "superior," "equal," or "inferior" in relation to oneself—to one's own "I"-concept. On account of the imaginative activity of wrong view (*diṭṭhi-maññanā*), in keeping with the initial distortion of perception, this distorted perception and the conclusions based on the imaginative activity of conceit are vividly imagined to be real. The imaginative activity of craving emerges repeatedly and enjoys the imaginings of conceit and views based on the wrong notion of "I." It enjoys them and becomes immersed in them. Craving further imagines it can possess the sense object as "mine" and retain it forever.[12] The cumulative effect of these imaginative activities, which can be mutually conditioning in various ways, is the firm stabilization of the concept "I am" within the mind.[13]

For the worldling, whose mind is enveloped on all sides by the darkness of ignorance, at least one of the imaginings of craving, conceit, or view will occur whenever he cognizes sense objects. Considered in this light it will become clear how strongly the concept of "I am" has become entrenched in the deluded mind. Consequently, a strong belief becomes firmly settled in the mind to the effect that there truly is an "I," a permanent and substantial entity which sees, hears, smells, tastes, feels, thinks, perceives, experiences, activates the body, and controls both the mind and the body. We imagine this "I" to be a sovereign and independent unit divorced from the external world. We develop a strong attachment towards this "I," take great interest in maintaining and protecting it, long to satisfy its desires. We struggle to accumulate all types of animate and inanimate possessions "for myself"; we hold tightly to opinions, views, and concepts which we consider "mine." It can be stated without any doubt that these twin concepts of "I" and "mine" are the root cause of all the world's problems, conflicts, divisions, and quarrels, both individually and collectively.

"I am" is a perverted notion, an imagining, generated in relation to all the five aggregates in general.[14] This can be explained as the initial stage of the self-view.[15]

(ii) *The imagining "I am this" (ayaṁ ahaṁ asmi)*

The unenlightened worldling, who relishes his deep attachment to the initial imagining "I am," eagerly seeks further confirmation of this vague "I"-concept. Conceiving it as a "self" endowed with attributes familiar to him through experience, he confers on it a definite form.[16] He confirms his imagined view "This I am" as follows: He imagines the aggregate of material form by identifying some particular internal or external material form thus: "This is what I am; this is my self"; the aggregate of feeling, by imagining: "It is this I, my self, that feels"; the aggregate of perception, by imagining: "It is this I, my self, that perceives"; the aggregate of mental formations, by imagining: "It is this I, my self, that activates the body and accumulates kamma," etc.; the aggregate of consciousness, by imagining: "It is this I, my self, that knows."[17] In keeping with the imagined view (*diṭṭhi-maññanā*) "This is my self" (*eso me attā*), there also sets in the function of the imaginative activity of conceit (*māna-maññanā*), which thinks "This I am" (*eso'ham asmi*), and the imaginative activity of craving (*taṇhā-maññanā*), which thinks "This is mine" (*etaṁ mama*).[18]

It is one or another of the five aggregates—or the five aggregates as a whole—that is knowingly or unknowingly conceived as a self in this manner.[19] This view of self—which can develop in any of four available modes in relation to each of the five aggregates—is referred to as "personality view" or the "false view of individuality" (*sakkāya-diṭṭhi*). It is on this basis that people firmly adhere to the diverse religious and philosophical beliefs confirming the concept of a self.[20]

(iii) *Imaginings regarding the future*

In a world that is impermanent, uncertain, and incomprehensible, the self that is imagined on the basis of the premise "This I am" offers the unenlightened worldling a delusive sense of security and stability.[21] As a result, he eagerly embraces the notion of self and engages in speculation about the future of this self in divergent ways to the extent that his powers of imagination permit.[22] If he tenaciously adopts the hypothesis, "My self is everlasting; I shall exist eternally (*bhavissaṁ*)," this amounts to the view of eternalism (*sassata-diṭṭhi*).[23] By speculating further regarding the nature of such an everlasting self, the following imaginings will occur to him: "I shall possess material form" (*rūpī bhavissaṁ*); "I shall be formless" (*arūpī bhavissaṁ*); "I shall be conscious" (*saññī bhavissaṁ*); "I shall be unconscious" (*asaññī bhavissaṁ*); "I shall be neither conscious nor unconscious" (*n'eva saññī nāsaññī bhavissaṁ*).[24]

If he adopts the hypothesis, "My self will terminate at death; I shall not exist in the future (*na bhavissaṁ*)," this amounts to the view of annihilationism (*uccheda-diṭṭhi*). This view is less appealing than eternalism, but is favoured by those who feel oppressed, humiliated, and repelled by existence. These people find delight in the annihilationist view and "overshoot" the path to Nibbāna by proclaiming: "Friend, this self, with the breakup of the physical body, disintegrates, is annihilated and destroyed, and does not exist any more after death. Such a condition would be serene, excellent, the true reality."[25]

In this way, once he has accepted the thesis that there is a self, the worldling bolsters the notion of self by adopting a theoretical view to explain the self's nature and destiny: either the view of eternalism, which affirms the eternal existence of the self; or the view of annihilationism, which denies the self a future beyond death.[26]

In the Yavakalāpī Sutta the Buddha has demonstrated that all terms pertaining to "I" or "self" are mere figments of one's imagination, offshoots of the defilements of craving, conceit, and view, propelled by ignorance. In instructing us to keep our minds free from such reckless ideas by treating them as snares of Māra, as diseases, boils, and darts, the Buddha has exposed the vanity, the danger, and the root cause of the doctrine of self along with the way to achieve freedom from it.[27]

It seems that even those who are not attached to the doctrine of self as a religious tenet still find it difficult to realize the truth of non-self, for they remain strongly influenced by the "I"-concept, the pre-theoretical imagining "I am." When a vessel or some precious utensil breaks, people find consolation by reminding themselves of the characteristic of impermanence. At funerals they always recite, "Subject to decay, alas, are all formations," and when they are stricken by illness or grief, they remind themselves of the characteristic of suffering. People console themselves in misfortune or distress by referring to both impermanence and suffering. But there is hardly anyone on such occasions who refers to the characteristic of non-self!

If we view life with an investigating mind, we will not find it too difficult to obtain a certain degree of conviction about the truth of non-self. We always want to continue living in good health, we wish to remain young, and we want to enhance and preserve our happiness. We do not like to fall ill, to grow old, to suffer, or to die. Nevertheless, despite such desires, everything we seek to avoid eventually catches up with us: we fall ill, we grow old, we suffer, and we will certainly die. Doesn't this show that there is no self regulating our lives or exercising authority over our minds and bodies? Just imagine yourself to be seriously ill or in an advanced state of senility. Then your hands and feet are not amenable to your control. Even your eyes, ears, and nose refuse to obey you. And very often the mind, too, is not under your command. Could this happen if there were an "I" exercising authority over your body and mind?

The following four factors too will be helpful in understanding the characteristic of non-self in the five aggregates:

1. Owing to the absence of an indwelling soul, an agent, an experiencer, or a supervisor within the five aggregates, they are void.
2. As no one has ownership over the five aggregates, they are ownerless.

3. There is no domination or mastery over the characteristic of change inherent in the five aggregates.
4. They preclude the nature of a self, i.e. of the hypothetical self accepted by the adherents of other belief systems.[28]

The Mark of Non-self in Insight Meditation

Now let us consider how the characteristic of non-self emerges in insight meditation. The meditator who has achieved purification of mind has thereby made the mind serene. Now it is workable to the extent that mindfulness and awareness can be successfully applied. Let us suppose that the meditator has chosen the rise and fall of the abdomen as his primary subject of meditation. With full concentration he directs his attention to the abdominal movement, and therein he clearly distinguishes the nature of motion, the air element (*vāyo-dhātu*). At times he might feel a sensation of heat within, which is the fire element (*tejo-dhātu*). Or he might experience a hard sensation of support, the earth element (*paṭhavī-dhātu*); or a cohesive or flowing sensation, the water element (*āpo-dhātu*).[29] Presently he realizes that there is a faculty knowing each of these objects—consciousness (*viññāṇa*); the encounter between the knowing faculty and the object—contact (*phassa*); the experiencing of the object's "flavour"—feeling (*vedanā*); the perceiving of the object—perception (*saññā*); the intentional mental activity regarding the object—volition (*cetanā*); the advertence of the mind to the object—attention (*manasikāra*).

In this way, as he comprehends these formations in their true nature, it becomes clear to him that there are two categories of phenomena: (i) those whose nature it is to cognize objects, i.e. the mental phenomena (*nāma-dhammā*) such as contact, feeling, perception, volition, and consciousness, which are capable of taking objects; and (ii) those whose nature it is not to cognize objects, the material phenomena (*rūpa-dhammā*) such as the elements of earth, water, heat, and air, which are incapable of taking objects.

By classifying the mental phenomena further into the categories of consciousness, feeling, perception, and mental formations (i.e. the remaining mental phenomena headed by volition), and by then combining them with material form, he will be able to comprehend them as the five aggregates. He will also understand how these five aggregates are interrelated.[30]

This is the stage of knowledge of delimitation of mentality and materiality (*nāmarūpapariccheda-ñāṇa*). Once this knowledge begins to function properly, the meditator's mind will shift away from conventional entities and become established in the ultimate realities—the mental and material phenomena. He also knows that all the objects impinging on the six sense faculties, even those external to his main subject of meditation, are just mental and material phenomena. As ignorance is held in check and wise attention comes to the fore, there will be no scope for distorted perceptions to arise in regard to mental and material phenomena, and as a result the imagination cannot find any chance to speculate about the self. The meditator will personally realize that there is no entity of any kind that can be, or should be, treated as "I" or "mine." He does not see an "I" or a "self" or "a being," but merely bare mental and material phenomena. He realizes there is no doer, no experiencer, no thinker, no perceiver, no ego dwelling within. The perception of self that had appeared so solid all along now melts away and the nature of non-self emerges. He confirms for himself, as personal knowledge, the right view that "in reality there are only mental and material phenomena but not a self, a being, or a person—no truly existent 'I.'" This fulfils the purification of view (*diṭṭhi-visuddhi*).

With the further refinement of mindfulness and awareness, and with the bolstering of concentration, the meditator realizes that different mental and material phenomena come into existence owing to the efficacy of their own appropriate causes. He understands that material phenomena are produced by causes and conditions such as ignorance, craving, kamma, nutriment, mind, and the heat element. He also discerns the causes for the generation of mental phenomena. He comprehends the doctrine of dependent arising (*paṭicca samuppāda*) in diverse ways and realizes the uninterrupted occurrence of the continuity of mental and material phenomena on the basis of the cause-and-effect relationship. By inference from his direct cognition of the present, he concludes that even in the past such a process of bare mental and material phenomena occurred, interconnected by the principle of cause and effect. He also comprehends that even in the future it will be so. He realizes: "There is no creator, sustainer, or destroyer of the world, yet the world does not come into being causelessly. There is no self-sufficient soul arising and subsisting independent of conditions. Mere natural phenomena alone occur by way of causes and effects."

All theories about the self generated through ignorance of dependent arising evaporate like dew at sunrise, replaced by the exclusive perception of non-self. Through realization that in all the three times—the past, the present, and the future—there is no permanent person designated "I" but only a continuum of phenomena linked as causes and effects, the meditator frees himself from all doubts pertaining to the three times, such as: "Was I in the past?" or "Am I at present?" or "Will I be in the future?" Accordingly, this stage is referred to as purification by overcoming doubt (*kaṅkhā-vitaraṇa-visuddhi*).

As mindfulness and awareness develop further, the meditator will discern in outline the origination and dissolution of the various groups of mental and material phenomena that he had comprehended in their occurrence by way of cause and effect. By collecting them into groups, he ascertains that all mental and material phenomena are impermanent as follows:

"Past material forms disappeared in the past itself; they did not proceed to the present; therefore past material forms are impermanent. Present material forms undergo destruction in the present itself; they shall not proceed to the future; therefore present material forms are impermanent. Future material forms will disappear in the future itself; therefore they too are impermanent. Those internal material forms belonging to my combination of five aggregates will undergo destruction internally; therefore they are impermanent. All other material forms external to them will undergo destruction externally; therefore they too are impermanent."

The same pattern of reflection is then extended to the phenomena included in the four mental aggregates. He then concludes that these mental and material phenomena, being subject to continuous destruction, are of a frightful nature and thus have the characteristic of suffering. Eventually he concludes that these mental and material phenomena, treated in groups as described above, are of the nature of non-self. For mental and material phenomena which are impermanent and suffering have no essence of their own; they are not under one's sway; they are devoid of a self.

In this manner the repeated contemplation of the characteristic of non-self uncovered in diverse ways is the contemplation of non-self. By this method the erroneous perception of self will be replaced by the correct perception of non-self.[31]

When the clear conviction dawns that each and every object entering through the six sense doors appears only to disappear in the very present, the meditator further verifies that there is no permanent essence in the five aggregates that can be grasped as a "self" or an "I." The insight into the origination of the aggregates will clearly convince the meditator of the hollowness of the view of annihilationism (*uccheda-diṭṭhi*), while insight into the dissolution of the aggregates will convince him of the vanity of the view of eternalism (*sassata-diṭṭhi*). He will come to understand that there is no self whatsoever that has any power over the incessant rising and passing away of the aggregates. He also will realize that the impermanent and painful aggregates cannot belong to a permanent self. The contemplation of non-self will gradually assume greater depth and, in combination with the contemplations of impermanence and suffering, will help to uncover the successive stages of insight knowledge.

Contemplation of non-self can be especially helpful in consolidating the knowledge of equanimity towards formations (*saṅkhār'upekkhā-ñāṇa*). Equanimity towards formations becomes established only when their voidness or nature of non-self is fully comprehended. Realization will come that these formations, which are devoid of any being, person, or self, are mere elements or activities, powerless and helpless. Moreover, it is only with the consummate realization of the knowledge of equanimity towards all formations that one becomes capable of renouncing all formations and directing the mind to Nibbāna. If the contemplation of non-self comes to the fore during the knowledge of conformity (*anuloma-ñāṇa*)—the next knowledge to arise in the series—it becomes the door to the void-liberation (*suññatā-vimokkha-mukha*) and accordingly reveals a vision of Nibbāna in its aspect of voidness (*suññatā*).

Like the deluded notions of permanence and pleasure, the concept of self too grows in three successive stages: by way of perception, consciousness, and view (*saññā, citta, diṭṭhi*). Along with the total elimination of the underlying tendency to views (*diṭṭhānusaya*) by the attainment of stream-entry (*sotāpatti*), these three stages of distortion (*vipallāsa*) are all extirpated simultaneously.[32] Yet, as the underlying tendency to the conceit "I am" (*mānānusaya*) persists, the notion "I am" will linger even in the noble disciple's mind until it is extricated by the path of arahantship. Although it is not a deeply rooted attachment like a full-fledged view (*diṭṭhi*), this conceit "I am" is still capable of functioning like a view in so far as it affirms the ego, though in a subdued way.[33]

* * *

> "O monks, when a monk sees six benefits, it should be enough for him to establish the perception of non-self towards all phenomena without exception. What six?
>
> 1. 'I shall be unidentified with anything in the world.'
> 2. 'Egotism will cease in me.'
> 3. 'Possessiveness will cease in me.'
> 4. 'I shall become endowed with an uncommon knowledge.'
> 5. 'Causal phenomena will be thoroughly seen by me.'
> 6. 'Causally arisen phenomena will be thoroughly seen by me.'"[34]

4

Contemplation of Revulsion (*Nibbidānupassanā*)

One who develops the contemplation of revulsion abandons delight.

(*Nibbidānupassanaṁ bhāvento nandiṁ pajahati.*)

How Revulsion Emerges in Insight Meditation

The term *nibbidā* means revulsion or disenchantment. In insight meditation this revulsion emerges in relation to formations, the phenomena of the five aggregates. When the true nature of formations is realized through insight knowledge, the delight (*nandi*) that the worldly mind takes in formations subsides and revulsion then emerges.[1]

In order to drive this point home the Buddha once cited the following parable to the wandering ascetic Māgandiya:[2]

> A person who had been blind from birth heard people say, "A white cloth is very attractive, clean and pleasant." Accordingly he desired to obtain a white cloth. A certain man learned of this and brought him a dark piece of coarse cloth, soiled with oil and soot. When handing it over to him, he praised it, saying: "Friend, this is a white cloth—pleasant, good, beautiful, and clean. Wear this and it will make you appear much more dignified." The blind man accepted it quite happily, put it on, and went about proudly, praising his so-called beautiful white cloth. Later his relatives and friends took him to an eye surgeon who restored his sight. After seeing his beloved white cloth with his own eyes, he understood that he had been cheated.

> Immediately, he abandoned his love for the cloth and became repelled by it.

In like manner the meditator who develops the eye of insight knowledge sees the true nature of the five aggregates and realizes that all this time he had been deluded into taking them as permanent, pleasurable, and self. With the deepening of insight he drains off delight in all formations and establishes himself solely in revulsion.

How revulsion emerges in insight meditation has been explained in many different ways in the scriptures. Let us now consider a few basic passages, in the Buddha's own words, on the transition from insight to revulsion:

> (i) "Monks, material form is impermanent, feeling is impermanent, perception is impermanent, mental formations are impermanent, consciousness is impermanent; the instructed noble disciple, endowed with this insight, develops revulsion towards the five aggregates—towards material form, feeling, perception, mental formations, and consciousness...."[3]

> (ii) "Monks, material form is impermanent; whatever is impermanent is suffering; whatever is suffering is non-self; whatever is non-self is not mine, not I, not my self. In this manner one should understand all material form in its true nature with insight knowledge. In like manner one should understand feeling, perception, mental formations, and consciousness. Accordingly, monks, the instructed noble disciple, endowed with this insight, cultivates revulsion towards each of these five aggregates."[4]

> (iii) "Monks, material form of the past and of the future is impermanent. What to speak of the present form? (It is certainly impermanent.) Monks, the instructed noble disciple, endowed with this insight, abandons interest in

the past material form; he does not wish for the future material form; he practises the way for revulsion, non-attachment, and cessation regarding the present material form. And so too for the aggregates of feeling, perception, mental formations, and consciousness pertaining to the three times."[5]

(iv) "Monks, material form is impermanent. Whatever be the cause or the condition for the arising of material form, that too is impermanent. Monks, how can material form, which is born from what is impermanent, be permanent? The other four aggregates are similarly impermanent. Monks, the instructed noble disciple, endowed with this insight, develops revulsion towards all the five aggregates."[6]

(v) "Monks, the instructed noble disciple contemplates wisely and thoroughly the principle of dependent arising thus: 'When this (cause) exists, that (result) comes to be; with this (cause) arising, that (result) arises. When this (cause) does not exist, that (result) does not come to be; with the cessation of this (cause), that (result) ceases; namely, through ignorance are conditioned the formations; through formations is conditioned consciousness ... through birth are conditioned decay and death, sorrow, lamentation, pain, grief, and despair. Such is the origin of this whole mass of suffering. By the complete cessation of ignorance, the formations cease ... and through the cessation of birth comes the cessation of decay and death, sorrow, lamentation, pain, grief, and despair. Thus comes about the cessation of this whole mass of suffering.' Monks, the instructed noble disciple, endowed with this insight, develops revulsion towards material form ... towards consciousness...."[7]

(vi) "Monks, here the instructed noble disciple reflects wisely and thoroughly on dependent arising thus: 'In this manner, when this exists, that comes to be ... with the cessation of this, that ceases.' Pleasurable feeling is produced through its condition, an appropriate contact; through the cessation of that same contact there also comes about the cessation, the allayment, of its own product, the pleasurable feeling. Painful feeling is produced through its condition, an appropriate contact; through the cessation of that same contact there also comes about the cessation, the allayment, of its own product, the painful feeling. Neutral feeling (neither pleasure nor pain) is produced through its condition, an appropriate contact; through the cessation of that same contact there also comes about the cessation, the allayment, of its own product, the neutral feeling.

"Monks, just as heat is produced by the friction and abrasion of two sticks, and that heat ceases and comes to an end by the separation and disconnection of the sticks, even so the pleasurable feeling, etc., is produced through its condition, an appropriate contact, and ceases through the cessation of that contact.... Monks, the instructed noble disciple, seeing thus, develops revulsion towards contact, feeling, perception, mental formations, and consciousness...."[8]

(vii) "Monks, because of the eye and visible forms there arises eye-consciousness. The coming together of these three (i.e. eye, forms, and eye-consciousness) is contact. Through contact there arises feeling. Monks, the instructed noble disciple, endowed with this insight, develops revulsion towards the eye, towards forms, towards eye-consciousness, towards eye-contact, and towards the associated feeling. Similarly, he develops revulsion towards the ear, sound, and ear-consciousness; towards the nose, smell, and nose-consciousness; towards the tongue, taste, and tongue-consciousness; towards the body, touch, and body-consciousness; towards the mind, mental objects, and mind-consciousness, and towards the respective contacts and the associated feelings."[9]

(viii) "Rāhula, the instructed noble disciple (who has seen with insight the sense faculties and their related formations as impermanent, suffering, and non-self) develops revulsion towards the eye, the visible form, eye-consciousness, eye-contact, and also towards any feeling, perception, mental formations, or consciousness conditioned by eye-contact. And so too for the other senses."[10]

(ix) "Monks, everything is burning. And what is everything that is burning? Monks, the eye is burning, visible forms are burning, eye-consciousness is burning, eye-contact is burning: whatever feeling, pleasant, painful, or neutral, is generated through eye-contact, all that too is burning. Burning with what? All that, I declare, is burning with the fire of lust, the fire of hatred, and the fire of delusion—burning with birth, decay, death, sorrow, lamentation, pain, grief, and despair. The ear is burning ... The nose ... The tongue ... The body ... The mind is burning ... burning with the fire of lust, the fire of hatred, and the fire of delusion....

"Monks, seeing thus the instructed noble disciple feels revulsion towards the eye, towards forms, towards eye-consciousness, towards eye-contact, and also towards the pleasant, painful, or neutral feelings generated through eye-contact ... towards the mind ... or neutral feelings generated through mind-contact."[11]

(x) "Rādha, when material form is present, death will be present, the killer and the one who dies also will be present. Therefore, Rādha, you should regard material form as death, as the killer, or as the one who dies: regard it as a disease, as a boil, as a dart, as a misfortune, as a source of misfortune. Those who regard material form in this manner regard it rightly.... And so too for feeling, perception, mental formations, and consciousness."

"Venerable sir, what is the purpose in regarding it rightly?"

"Rādha, regarding it rightly is for the purpose of revulsion."[12]

(xi) "Rāhula, is the earth element permanent or impermanent?"

"Venerable sir, it is impermanent."

"If a thing is impermanent, is it painful or pleasant?"

"Venerable sir, it is painful."

"If a thing is impermanent, painful, and changeable, is it proper to consider it as 'this is mine,' 'this I am,' or 'this is my self'?"

"Venerable sir, it is not proper."

(Having pointed out in the same way the three characteristics in the other elements—water, fire, air, space, and consciousness—the Buddha continues thus:)

"Rāhula, seeing thus through insight, the wise noble disciple feels revulsion towards the elements of earth, water, heat, air, space, and consciousness."[13]

(xii) "O monk, if one lives contemplating continuously the rise and fall of the eye-faculty, one feels revulsion towards the eye-faculty. Similarly if one lives contemplating continuously the rise and fall of the sense faculties of ear, nose, tongue, body, or mind, one feels revulsion towards each of them."[14]

The Development of Revulsion

Although the Buddha has taught in many different ways in keeping with the mentality of each of his disciples, when we collate these different expositions of the Dhamma it becomes possible for us to define a common programme of action for the development of revulsion. The fundamentals of such a system of insight development can be briefly explained thus:

1. One first comprehends the mental and material phenomena in their different categories as aggregates, bases, elements, or faculties, according to the capacity of each meditator. This is the comprehension of individual characteristics (*paccattalakkhaṇa-paṭivedha*).
2. One then realizes that all formations understood in the aforesaid manner are linked by the law of cause and effect (*paccaya-pariggaha*).
3. One next realizes that all these causal and resultant phenomena are subject to the three common characteristics of impermanence, suffering, and non-self, and therefore are sources of danger.

The clear understanding of the dangers in formations—their being beset by the three characteristics—functions as the immediate cause for the generation of revulsion.[15]

In many discourses (mainly in the Aṅguttara Nikāya) the Buddha states that the foundation for revulsion is correct knowledge and vision (*yathābhūta-ñāṇadassana*), which in turn is the result of right concentration.[16] The phrase *yathābhūta-ñāṇadassana* conveys the idea of seeing reality with insight knowledge. This single phrase summarizes all the three stages given above as the foundation of revulsion.[17] The commentaries explain "correct knowledge and vision" as "tender insight" (*taruṇa-vipassanā*) and revulsion as "strong insight" (*balava-vipassanā*).[18]

The repeated application of attention and insight-wisdom for the development of revulsion generated through insight is the contemplation of revulsion (*nibbidānupassanā*). It is only by the uninterrupted and sustained application of wise attention that the contemplation of revulsion can succeed. When the mind is distracted concentration falters. Interruptions make mindfulness and concentration slack, and consequently the mental process cannot acquire the strong focus needed to contemplate the three characteristics. The development of contemplation consists simply in steering the mind in a direction conducive to the emergence and development of mindfulness, concentration, and wisdom.

With the gradual maturation of the three contemplations of impermanence, suffering, and non-self, the perilous nature of conditioned phenomena becomes evident. This generates revulsion towards formations. This contemplation of revulsion develops gradually. When the knowledge of the dissolution of formations (*bhaṅga-ñāṇa*) sets in, the contemplation of revulsion also gathers sufficient power to subdue delight.[19] From this point on the contemplation gradually gains momentum, reaching its climax with the dawning of the insight knowledge of revulsion (*nibbidā-ñāṇa*). Thereafter, when the knowledge of equanimity towards formations (*saṅkhār'upekkhā-ñāṇa*) is attained, the contemplation of revulsion recedes.[20] Delight, as well as any semblance of revulsion, will disappear and the meditation of insight will continue in a serene and dispassionate manner.

The contemplation of revulsion assumes a place of paramount significance in insight meditation. The greater the revulsion, the easier the abandonment of formations. Through the complete abandonment of formations one will realize Nibbāna. For those fortunate people sufficiently advanced in their journey towards arahantship—those whose spiritual faculties have reached a high degree of maturity through the prolonged practice of tranquillity and insight meditation in their previous lives—revulsion may set in immediately and intensively through a deep realization of the three characteristics. They will be able to attain the consummation of insight meditation quickly without need to spend much time on the contemplation of revulsion.[21]

A lofty individual with a well-developed mind might bring forth intense revulsion even in regard to a sense object that normally rouses passion. One example of this is the case of the Elder Nāgasamāla. Once, as he entered the city for alms, this elder saw a nautch girl performing in public to the accompaniment of music. She was attractively dressed with sandalwood cream applied on her body and decked with ornaments and flower garlands. But to the elder she appeared as nothing other than a well-devised death trap set up by Māra the Evil One. As he developed wise attention the dangers of formations became doubly clear to him and intense revulsion set in. Then, right on the spot, the elder attained arahantship along with the three higher knowledges.[22]

The meditator not endowed with such a high degree of innate mental strength has to apply wise attention repeatedly in such a way that revulsion is cultivated and brought to the required degree of intensity.

The contemplation of revulsion is the outcome of the three preceding contemplations, but by its own intrinsic nature it should be regarded as a special form of the contemplation of suffering. This is also implied by the fact that the delight it eliminates is closely related to the perception of pleasure that is eliminated by the contemplation of suffering.

Revulsion and Delight

At this point in our inquiry it is pertinent to discuss the role of delight (*nandi*). Delight is craving accompanied by zest.[23] It is the habit of enjoying formations gleefully and avariciously under the delusion that they are "I" or "mine," taking them, through ignorance of their true nature, to be pleasing, welcome, agreeable, and pleasurable. Let us now turn our attention to a discourse of the Buddha which shows how delight originates and leads to bitter consequences:

> "Having seen a pleasant form, he becomes attached to it; when the form is unpleasant he detests it; ignorant of the true nature of the body he lives with unwholesome

> thoughts. He is ignorant of that heart-deliverance and wisdom-deliverance (the fruition of arahantship), wherein such evil, unwholesome thoughts utterly cease. While confronted with this ambivalence of compliance and conflict, whatever feeling he experiences, whether pleasant, painful, or neutral, he welcomes it. Conditioned by his craving, he now thinks, 'It is I, it is mine'; and he immerses himself in that feeling with a degree of craving so intense that escape from it becomes almost impossible.
>
> To one who finds pleasure in this feeling, who immerses himself in it calling it 'I' and 'mine,' there arises delight (*nandi*). When delight arises in relation to any kind of feeling the result is clinging (*upādāna*). This in turn conditions becoming (*bhava*). Becoming conditions birth, which conditions decay and death, sorrow, lamentation, pain, grief, and despair. In this manner there arises this entire mass of suffering. Having heard a sound ... Having smelt an odour ... Having experienced a taste ... Having experienced a touch ... Having thought of a mental object ... In this manner there arises ... suffering."[24]

Just ponder for a moment how many of your daily activities are imbued with this delight, which arises when you fail to set up wise attention and awareness over the acts of consciousness occurring at the six sense faculties. Every time you lose restraint over your sense faculties this delight is generated, driving you into future existences where you will undergo a vast mass of suffering in the form of birth, decay, and death, sorrow and grief, illness and stress. By contemplating this fact you can bring forth a keen sense of urgency and devote yourself to the contemplation of revulsion with intensified earnestness.

The meditator who engages in insight meditation with a concentrated mind comprehends the process of sense perception in its true nature. He fully realizes that what takes place at all times is just the continuous functioning of a group of mental and material phenomena on the basis of the cause-and-effect relationship. He also realizes that each of these formations is subject to momentary origination and cessation, that they are stressful, and also that they are totally devoid of any inner core of a self. He comprehends the dangers involved in formations in diverse ways. At this stage the relishing of formations that had become entrenched in his mind, along with the habit of gleefully welcoming them, begins to slip away. In their place revulsion towards formations sets in and gathers momentum. Nothing is selfishly adhered to as "I" or "mine." One does not adhere to worldly enjoyments. The delight is subdued by the matured revulsion in exactly the same way as the blind man, on gaining his eyesight, loses interest in the loathsome piece of cloth which until then he had clasped with so much love and care.

With the gradual development of the contemplation of revulsion, the meditator will begin to abhor even the realms of gods and Brahmās. Feelings of delight relating to the sensuous, fine-material, and immaterial spheres will dry up. The meditator will begin to make statements like the following: "At first I wanted only to free myself from the realms of misery, but now this entire triple world appears as one whole conflagration, a heap of suffering. I have no liking for any form of becoming." His mind has no more room for worldly thoughts of enjoyment. A strong urge to free himself from all defilements becomes established.[25]

When the contemplation of revulsion is extended in this manner to all internal and external phenomena, certain meditators tend to become confused. Here a meditator loses interest in everything, including such essential activities as partaking of food or performing the daily chores. He feels driven to change his clothing and seat constantly. He might begin to dislike his cell or home, his meditation cushion, or even his meditation master. He might even feel compelled to give up everything and wander aimlessly. Yet for all that, he is never prompted to give up meditation.

If such a situation arises, one should confide it to the meditation master or to an experienced meditator without concealing anything. One should recognize that while this disenchantment arises in relation to formations, the correct course of action is that of continuing with the meditation uninterruptedly. By thus remaining engaged in the unimpeded contemplation of revulsion, a stage will be reached when this revulsion ceases and the mind becomes exceedingly peaceful.

* * *

> "O monks, I declare that when one lives engaged in the contemplation of revulsion towards things that fetter, one abandons lust, hatred, and delusion. By abandoning lust, hatred, and delusion one achieves freedom from the suffering of repeated birth, decay and death, sorrow, lamentation, pain, grief, and despair."[26]

5

Contemplation of Dispassion (*Virāgānupassanā*)

> One who develops the contemplation of dispassion abandons passion.
>
> (*Virāgānupassanaṁ bhāvento rāgaṁ pajahati.*)

The Meaning of Dispassion

The term *virāga,* which generally means dispassion or non-attachment, has been used in various senses in the texts.[1] A few of the meanings relevant to the present context are the following:

1. The "fading away" or removal of passion and lust towards formations, which is achieved by means of insight wisdom through the method of "substitution of opposites"; because dispassion replaces passion in the course of contemplation, this could be referred to as "substitutional dispassion" (*tadaṅga-virāga*).[2]
2. The momentary dissolution of formations, called "destructional dispassion" (i.e. "destruction as a form of dispassion" or "fading away by destruction," *khaya-virāga*).[3]
3. Nibbāna, which is the ultimate dispassion (*accanta-virāga*) or emancipatory dispassion (*nissaraṇa-virāga*).[4]
4. The supramundane path, which uproots passion permanently and thus may be called extirpative dispassion (*samuccheda-virāga*).[5]

It appears that the first definition of dispassion here—i.e. the fading away of passion as a consequence of insight—best describes the contemplation of dispassion as understood in the context of the seven contemplations.[6] As such, we shall delineate the contemplation of dispassion on the basis of that definition while at the same time relating the discussion to the other meanings as well.

The Contemplation of Dispassion

The contemplation of dispassion does not become manifest until one reaches the mature insight knowledge regarding rise and fall. When this deep knowledge becomes activated, the meditator clearly grasps the three characteristics of phenomena, and this knowledge serves as a condition for the partial occurrence of the contemplation of revulsion as well. Simultaneously, there sets in non-attachment towards formations. The contemplation of dispassion through the substitution of opposites is the application of insight contemplation to facilitate the development of this non-attachment.

At this stage, even though the meditator clearly grasps both the rise and fall of phenomena, as a result of this "contemplation of dispassion through the substitution of opposites" his attention fixes more intently upon their fall than upon their rise. As the falling away of formations becomes more prominent, contemplation of impermanence becomes sharper. This paves the way for the knowledge of dissolution (*bhaṅga-ñāṇa*), at which stage the meditator altogether abandons concern with the rise of formations and fixes his attention solely on their momentary dissolution. When this momentary dissolution is considered as "destructional dispassion," it can be seen how the contemplation of dispassion gathers momentum through the repeated observation of "destructional dispassion."

When the meditator sees how all the mental and material

formations that become the objects of the mind—along with those very states of mind that perform the contemplation—are constantly breaking up and dissolving, he comprehends the great fearfulness in the world of formations. Also, by contemplating how formations are always fading away by destruction, their manifold dangers become evident. As a result, the contemplation of revulsion emerges and gathers strength. The non-attachment that follows brings to prominence the contemplation of dispassion through the substitution of opposites. Although the contemplation of revulsion gradually subsides after the knowledge of revulsion has reached its consummation, the contemplation of dispassion continues to gain momentum. This contemplation of "substitutional dispassion" subdues passion and paves the way for the emergence of equanimity. It thereby becomes an immensely powerful supporting condition for the stage of insight knowledge called knowledge of equanimity towards formations (*saṅkhār'upekkhā-ñāṇa*) to arise. This itself is the forerunner to the emergence of the supramundane path process.

By this time the meditator has acquired an inferential knowledge that Nibbāna is the ultimate state of dispassion. While engaged in the contemplation of "destructional dispassion," i.e. contemplation of the momentary dissolution of phenomena, he has also realized: "Nibbāna, called the state of dispassion, is exceedingly serene and lofty, for it transcends the continuous dissolution of formations." While engaged in the contemplation of "dispassion through the substitution of opposites" it occurs to him: "Nibbāna, called the state of dispassion, is exceedingly serene and lofty, for it is entirely free from all formations and devoid of even a vestige of passion."[7] The repeated experience of this observation can also be identified as the contemplation of dispassion.

The consummation of insight is regarded as the acme of the contemplation of dispassion. When, through the successful fulfilment of the contemplation of dispassion, the meditator has suppressed passion for all formations by means of the substitution of opposites, with the utter relinquishing of all formations as objects he will directly experience Nibbāna, the ultimate state of dispassion. This supramundane path condition, known as "extirpative dispassion" or the extirpation of passion (*samuccheda-virāga*), is also described in the commentaries as a form of the contemplation of dispassion.[8]

Of the sixteen stages of mindfulness of breathing, the fourteenth is the contemplation of dispassion, which the *Paṭisambhidāmagga* describes in the following terms (the bracketed portions are from the commentary):

> Having seen [onwards from the knowledge of dissolution] the dangers involved in material form and endowed with a [wholesome] desire [generated by knowledge obtained from the scriptures] for dispassion towards material form (i.e. for Nibbāna), he decides on [that Nibbāna] with full confidence. The meditator's mind is also firmly established [in destructional dispassion, which is the destruction of material phenomena, as an object of the mind, and in Nibbāna, on the basis of the scriptures, which is the ultimate state of dispassion]. (In this manner) he trains himself repeatedly thus, "I shall breathe in contemplating dispassion towards material form; I shall breathe out contemplating dispassion towards material form." (This account is repeated in relation to the remaining four aggregates with "material form" replaced successively by feeling, perception, mental formations, and consciousness.)[9]

The *Visuddhimagga*, in defining the contemplation of dispassion as the same fourteenth stage in mindfulness of breathing, emphasizes dispassion as the momentary destruction of formations and remains silent on dispassion through the substitution of opposites.[10] The commentary to the *Paṭisambhidāmagga*, too, seems to have followed that tradition here. Yet, since the text contains the phrase "having seen the danger involved in material form," one can easily bring dispassion through the substitution of opposites into the context too, for it was shown earlier how revulsion and dispassion through the substitution of opposites follow when one comprehends the dangers in phenomena (see p.64 above). Dispassion through substitution, it should be noted, can also result from the contemplation of destructional dispassion, i.e. from contemplation of the momentary destruction of phenomena.[11]

Dispassion and Revulsion

The contemplation of revulsion that emerges from the realization of the dangers involved in formations, and the contemplation of dispassion that gathers momentum from this realization, are closely related.[12] The *Paṭisambhidāmagga Commentary* in one place has even identified the contemplation of dispassion with that of revulsion.[13] In some suttas the Buddha has joined the two terms "revulsion" and "dispassion" into the compound "revulsion-dispassion" (*nibbidā-virāga*).[14] Also, the contemplation referred to in the texts as "the perception of distaste for the whole world" (*sabbaloke anabhiratasaññā*) can be identified either as the contemplation of revulsion (which is preferred by the commentaries and the sub-commentaries) or as the contemplation of dispassion.[15]

The close similarity between delight (*nandi*) and passion (*rāga*), which are respectively eliminated by the contemplation of revulsion and that of dispassion, also confirms the similarity between these two contemplations. *Nandi* is the greed produced by delight, *rāga* the greed produced by attachment.[16] It is also stated that whereas *nandi* is craving accompanied by zest (*sappītika-taṇhā*), *rāga* is craving devoid of zest (*nippītika-taṇhā*).[17] Discourses are not uncommon in which *nandi* and *rāga* occur in the compound *nandi-rāga*: "Monks, one who contemplates material form and comprehends it as it really is in respect of its impermanence, develops revulsion towards material form. By the elimination of delight, passion is eliminated; by the elimination of passion, delight is eliminated. By the elimination of both delight and passion (*nandi-rāga*), the mind is completely liberated."[18] These words of the Buddha indicate underline the close link between *nandi* and *rāga*.

If that be so, are revulsion (*nibbidā*) and dispassion (*virāga*) identical? Though the two are very similar, other discourses of the Buddha indicate a difference, a cause-and-effect relationship, between them: "Monks, I declare that dispassion is with cause and not without cause. What is the cause of dispassion? It has to be stated: revulsion."[19]

Here the commentary describes revulsion as intensified insight and dispassion as the supramundane path.[20] In the discourses where revulsion and dispassion occur together (especially in places where the three stages of revulsion, dispassion, and liberation are cited in sequence), very often the commentary interprets dispassion as the supramundane path.[21] (Among the examples adduced in Chapter 4 for the divergent ways in which revulsion can emerge, all but one deal with the process from revulsion to dispassion and liberation.)

Nevertheless, there is evidence in the texts that dispassion following on revulsion need not always be supramundane. For instance, consider the following passage:

> "Monks, it is said that of all the inhabitants and rulers of Kāsi-Kosala, King Pasenadi is the foremost. Yet King Pasenadi is certainly subject to change, subject to death. Monks, the instructed noble disciple who comprehends this fact develops revulsion even towards kingship and becomes dispassionate (*virajjati*) even towards the foremost, the crown of Kosala. This being the case, what need is there to speak of those inferior sensual pleasures?"[22]

It is clear that "becomes dispassionate" (*virajjati*) here denotes a mundane variety of dispassion, and from this example and the others cited in the sutta it becomes plain that dispassion can be cultivated in relation even to the ordinary objects belonging to the external world.

In the Dhātuvibhaṅga Sutta, the Buddha explains how, in advanced insight, mundane dispassion is achieved immediately after revulsion. The detailed account of the meditation on elements given there can be summarized as follows:

> The meditator, with right insight knowledge, comprehends both the internal earth element and the external earth element as simply the earth element. He contemplates it as 'not mine, not I, not my self.' Thereby he develops revulsion towards the earth element and his mind becomes dispassionate towards it (i.e. he develops mundane dispassion). In like manner he develops revulsion and dispassion towards the elements of water, fire, air, and space. Now there remains only that consciousness, purified and resplendent. Through this consciousness he comes to understand that all feelings, whether pleasant, painful, or neutral, arise through contact and cease in the absence of contact.[23] Eventually he achieves equanimity (*upekkhā*), purified, pliable, amenable, and resplendent. He does not abuse this condition to accumulate formations that prolong the cycle of existence. Without grasping anything mundane, never incited by craving, he realizes arahantship by extinguishing the fires of passion (i.e. he experiences supramundane dispassion).[24]

Here it appears that dispassion towards the five material elements—earth, water, fire, air, and space—occurs at an elevated stage of insight meditation. Nevertheless, this must pertain to the mundane level because at the supramundane level dispassion towards both mind and matter together should occur simultaneously. The supramundane condition dawns only with the subsequent perfection of insight by extending it to embrace the mental phenomena as well. Hence it can be stated that the dispassion resulting from revulsion is initially a mundane condition and it is through further development that it attains to the supramundane level.[25]

The Maturation of Dispassion

This viewpoint receives confirmation when we inquire how the two contemplations of revulsion and of dispassion function in mutual association at the practical level. It is by seeing the dangers harboured in formations that revulsion is produced, and this in turn issues in dispassion. These two contemplations continue to develop in unison as a cause-and-effect nexus until they reach the acme of the knowledge of revulsion. At this stage it would be difficult to distinguish between the two as separate contemplations.

With the further development of insight and the consequent stabilization of the knowledge of equanimity towards formations, the contemplation of revulsion begins to decline as there is no further need for it.[26] Yet the contemplation of dispassion now exercises its function with still greater strength, tending more and more towards equanimity of insight, an evenness of mind free from all attachment and conflict, without a trace of revulsion.

Even at the stage of equanimity towards formations, the object of one's attention will be one of the three characteristics of phenomena. Yet what results from this will not be revulsion (as in the earlier phase) but sheer dispassion, a mature phase of dispassion that reveals itself as equanimity. In consequence, the contemplation of dispassion unfolds effortlessly. At this stage, however, although the contemplation of revulsion has faded out, it is due to the initial impetus imparted by the contemplation of revulsion that the contemplation of dispassion could achieve, in this later phase, the degree of intensity it now commands. Therefore it can be maintained that even this phase of the contemplation of dispassion is a product of the contemplation of revulsion.

Let us clarify this point with an illustration. Imagine a child is rolling a wheel along a straight road. Though the child and the wheel are both moving in unison, the wheel actually rolls on owing to the thrust imparted to it by the child. As the child gradually increases his speed, the wheel too accelerates. When the child is running at his topmost speed he comes to a decline in the road. Here he stops and allows the wheel to proceed on its own, as there is no further need for him to push it. However, the wheel rolls on down the decline with increasing speed because of the initial impetus given to it by the child. If we compare the child to the contemplation of revulsion, the wheel to the contemplation of dispassion, intensified insight meditation to the straight roadway, and the decline to the knowledge of equanimity towards formations, the meaning of the simile should be clear.

When equanimity towards formations is achieved the contemplation of dispassion reaches maturity. After this it issues in the supramundane path, whereby it acquires a supramundane quality. Accordingly it has to be stated that dispassion, realized as a fruit of revulsion, initially emerges on the mundane level and subsequently attains to the supramundane level, while revulsion itself always remains on the mundane level. We make this assertion on the premise that revulsion and dispassion are two contemplations that unfold gradually in intensified insight meditation, not by taking revulsion either as a broad term designating insight in general or as a special stage of insight knowledge called "knowledge of revulsion" (see Chap. 4, n.18).

Therefore, in the suttas which posit the stages of revulsion, dispassion, and liberation in causal sequence (see Chap. 4, n.21), if we bear in mind the functions of the contemplations of revulsion and of dispassion in the advanced insight meditation of the ordinary meditator, we cannot regard such dispassion as exclusively the supramundane state itself. It would be more reasonable to treat the term "dispassion" (*virāga*) here as embracing both the initial mundane stage of the contemplation of dispassion as well as its supramundane stage.

The Subduing of Passion

Since it is passion that is eliminated through the contemplation of dispassion, this contemplation can be regarded as a particular aspect of the contemplation of suffering, on the ground that the contemplation of suffering is an antidote to craving and passion is a synonym of craving. Yet when dispassion is interpreted as the momentary destruction of phenomena, it should be understood as an aspect of the contemplation of impermanence, i.e. as seeing repeatedly the momentary dissolution of formations. Further, by recognizing that dispassion through the substitution of opposites—i.e. the fading out of passion—can result from the contemplation of the momentary destruction of phenomena, we can again classify the contemplation of dispassion as a form of the contemplation of suffering.

Cogent evidence can also be cited from the *Paṭisambhidāmagga* to establish that the contemplation of dispassion in itself is directly an aspect of the contemplation of suffering. In the *Paṭisambhidā* we find a classification of contemplations on the basis of the type of clinging (*upādāna*) eliminated by each contemplation. According to this classification, the contemplations of impermanence, of non-self, and others of similar nature constitute one category, while those of suffering and others of similar nature constitute another category. The contemplation of revulsion and of dispassion are also included in the latter category, which eliminates only the "clinging to sensual pleasures."[27]

The lust or passion (*rāga*) that is eliminated through the contemplation of dispassion is indeed a defilement deeply rooted in the mind. It is owing to our passionate attachment and clinging to formations that we are trapped in this dreadful cycle of existence, wandering from one state of becoming to another. We can hardly conceive how tightly we have chained ourselves to the fetters of lust throughout this long, beginningless cycle of existence! "Lust destroys vision, lust destroys wisdom; it is on the side of suffering; it does not lead to Nibbāna."[28]

Correct knowledge and vision (*yathābhūta-ñāṇadassana*) arises by the proper practice of insight meditation. The meditator will realize directly that all formations are subject to origination and cessation and as such are mere natural phenomena devoid of any such essence as a self, a person, or a being; inevitably they bring suffering in their wake. He clearly discerns that there is nothing in them worth clinging to, nothing worth attaching oneself to, nothing worth hoping for. Consequently the passion ingrained in his mind becomes exhausted.

As the contemplation of dispassion progresses, the meditator will realize that he no longer experiences the attachments he formerly had towards the beauty, youthfulness, health, and strength of his physical body. He sees as vain all our efforts to adorn the body with lovely clothes, scents and cosmetics, unguents, and jewellery. The task of maintaining this worthless body, which is a heap of impurities, is felt as a heavy burden. One no longer entertains even the least urge to see attractive forms, to hear lovely sounds, to enjoy pleasant smells, to partake of tasty food, to enjoy pleasurable tactile sensations, or to wallow in passionate thoughts. All the old bonds of affection for persons and possessions are torn asunder. All expectations for gain, fame, property, power, and other mundane attainments drop away. Even the desire for future happiness in heavenly and earthly realms vanishes.

When the contemplation of dispassion reaches its culmination, passion becomes utterly subdued and the mind is completely purified. Even if one deliberately directs one's attention to desirable sense objects, no desire will emerge; the mind remains passionless. However, caution is needed here, for insight knowledge only suspends lust; it does not eradicate it. Because one's mind appears pure one might assume that one has attained to the paths and fruits and eliminated all defilements. However, because one has only temporarily removed the defilements through the substitution of opposites, if one were to stop insight meditation for a while one would observe how they return. Accordingly, if one grasps one's real situation with the help of the meditation master and continues with the meditation, one will in time experience the supramundane dispassion, the true goal of the practice.

*   *   *

> "Monks, the contemplation of dispassion, when developed and cultivated, brings about great fruit and great profit."[29]

6

Contemplation of Cessation (*Nirodhānupassanā*)

One who develops the contemplation of cessation abandons origination.

(*Nirodhānupassanaṁ bhāvento samudayaṁ pajahati.*)

The Meaning of Cessation

Cessation (*nirodha*) can be explained in three ways: (i) in terms of the person or entity that ceases; (ii) as the act of ceasing; or (iii) as the state of having ceased, i.e. the termination of continuity.[1] Let us examine the nature of cessation in relation to the present topic.

Venerable Ānanda, seated beside the Buddha, once put the following question to him:

> "Venerable sir, it is often said 'cessation, cessation.' What are the phenomena that should cease for this term 'cessation' to be used?"
>
> "Ānanda, material form is impermanent, conditioned, dependently arisen, subject to destruction, to fall, to breaking up, to ceasing. Because of its ceasing the word 'cessation' is used. Feeling is impermanent ... Perception is impermanent ... Mental formations are impermanent ... Consciousness is impermanent ... Because of its ceasing the word 'cessation' is used."[2]

Thus the term *nirodha* refers to the cessation, termination, dissolution, and stoppage of the conditioned formations comprised in the five aggregates. This cessation occurs in two main stages:

1. The first stage is the ordinary cessation of formations incessantly occurring in a way conditional to their continued emergence. This is the term "cessation leading to continued origination" (*uppāda-nirodha*). When the reference is to the momentary cessation of phenomena it is also designated "destructional cessation" (*khaya-nirodha* = cessation through destruction).[3]

2. The second stage is the extirpation of formations without any re-origination (*samuccheda-nirodha* or *anuppāda-nirodha*).[4] This stage is tantamount to the supramundane path, wherein Nibbāna is realized as the ultimate cessation (*accanta-nirodha*) or the emancipatory cessation (*nissaraṇa-nirodha*).[5]

In this examination of the contemplation of cessation much of our attention will be devoted to the momentary cessation of formations. The ultimate cessation, cessation without re-origination, will be treated as the special stage when the contemplation of cessation reaches its consummation.

The Emergence of Cessation

The contemplation of cessation is the repeated investigation of the cessation of formations with insight-wisdom.[6] This contemplation becomes manifest in varying forms in the course of insight meditation. Let us first explain, by means of an illustration, how it appears in its most rudimentary form.

The insight meditator who is observing the rise and fall of the abdomen as his primary subject of meditation gradually sharpens his mindfulness and concentration. As he does so, he becomes capable of clearly noticing the beginning and the end of each rise of the abdomen; he also considers that in between the beginning and the end of the rising movement is the middle stage of the rise. Immediately following the end of the rising movement, the falling movement begins, which ceases instantly, invariably followed by another rise. This, too, quickly ceases, followed by still another fall. By contemplating this process continuously with a concentrated mind the meditator reaches success in the contemplation of impermanence. In this phase of meditation, the precise and undeflected observation of the endpoints of each rise and fall can be considered the initial form of the contemplation of cessation.

As the meditator further refines his attention, his insight knowledge will enable him to discern a number of successive "minor rises" occurring within a single full rise of the abdomen. Each of these minor rises has its own origin and cessation, which in time become clear to the attentive meditator. So too, within each complete falling movement of the abdomen there occurs a number of successive "minor falls," each having its own origin and cessation. These, too, the meditator discerns. Gradually the meditator becomes capable of knowing directly, in the same manner, the continuous origin and cessation of all the objects of the six sense faculties. For instance, in place of what was previously cognized as a single unit of sound, he now perceives a series of discrete units of sound, each with its own origination and cessation. Even thoughts are clearly seen as arising and ceasing in serial succession. In this manner, as the contemplation of impermanence gradually deepens and intensifies, the knowledge of the rise and fall of phenomena dawns and comes to maturity, enabling the meditator to see clearly, at any given moment, how the entire phenomenal world is subject to the law of momentary origination and cessation. Along with the contemplation of impermanence, the contemplation of cessation too grows and develops concurrently.

At the next stage in the maturation of insight the contemplation of cessation comes to the fore. Now it is the cessation of formations rather than their origination that becomes prominent. The meditator will clearly comprehend how every formation that he attends to promptly dissolves as soon as it has arisen. Sometimes he may even get the impression that the object has already ceased before he has noted it. He also observes how the contemplating mind too breaks up in the very process of noting the dissolving object. The meditator might feel that his mindfulness has regressed, but in reality this is a sign of progress. By now he has transcended the knowledge of rise and fall and arrived at the knowledge of dissolution (*bhaṅga-ñāṇa*). At this stage the presently occurring momentary cessation of formations, in other words their cessation through dissolution (*khaya-nirodha*), will strongly impress itself on the meditator's mind. This constitutes an intensified stage in the contemplation of cessation.[7]

Through inferential knowledge the meditator will next realize that in the past too, in exactly the same way, formations were incessantly subject to dissolution, and that in the future too this momentary cessation will continue unabated.[8] He further realizes, with the force of direct cognition, that this is the fundamental nature of things, not only in his own five aggregates but throughout the entire triple world. Accordingly he penetrates the intensely frightening nature of formations, which brings the knowledge of appearance as terror (*bhayat' upaṭṭhāna-ñāṇa*). Likewise, he realizes in a variety of ways the extensive dangers involved in formations, i.e. knowledge of danger (*ādīnava-ñāṇa*).

Based on this he develops revulsion towards formations—knowledge of revulsion (*nibbidā-ñāṇa*). There arises in him a deep wish for the eternal allayment, the discontinuance, of this continuity of formations, which keep on ceasing incessantly.[9] Accordingly, when the meditator directly realizes cessation as the dissolution of formations, his attention repeatedly turns, by way of inferential knowledge, to Nibbāna as the ultimate cessation. This can be regarded as still another facet of the contemplation of cessation.[10] Conjoined with this contemplation, the wish to achieve deliverance from formations becomes stronger. Thus the meditator arrives at the knowledge of desire for deliverance (*muñcitukamyatā-ñāṇa*).[11]

At times the meditator's main meditation subject may vanish completely. The person who practises mindfulness of breathing ceases to feel the breath. One who attends to the rise and fall of the abdomen ceases to feel the rising and falling movement in the abdominal region. One who fixes attention on the posture of sitting loses the sense of the presence of the body. Occasionally one might even feel that one's head or some other part of one's body has vanished. One attending to the various touch sensations of the body might cease to experience tangibility. When the meditator developing the contemplation of elements analyses and separates them as earth, water, fire, and air, he may fail to discern the presence of his body. For some, the entire perception of material form ceases, leaving only the mental flux as the object of attention.[12] Contemplating the cessation of perception in regard to the different parts of the physical form can be adduced as yet another aspect of the contemplation of cessation.

When they lose perception of the main subject of meditation, some meditators are overcome by fear while others convince themselves that they have attained a supramundane realization. But such bizarre experiences are only incidental by-products marking some degree of progress in mundane insight. If the primary meditation subject disappears, the meditator should not allow either fear or pride to prevail. Instead, he should direct his attention to some other object that is clear to him. If no discernment of any material form is possible, he should fix his attention on his presently occurring continuity of consciousness. It is possible that while he is contemplating a different subject, the earlier subject of meditation may reappear; in such a case he should revert to that earlier subject. If he ceases to experience any object apprehended through the five sense doors, and instead experiences only the continuity of consciousness through the mind-door, such a condition should be regarded as an exalted mundane state of concentration.

As the meditator's concentration deepens, the cessation of every object of sense cognition becomes immediately apparent to him. He comprehends how, when a formation ceases, it ceases forever without any possibility of re-emergence. What emerges subsequently is an entirely new formation, which also fully ceases in an instant.[13] The contemplation of cessation, by engendering this direct realization of the momentary extirpation of every object cognized as well as of every cognizing mind state, clearly discloses the nature of non-self in regard to all formations. Presently, the meditator penetrates the following truth: If it is the case that all formations relating to the five aggregates completely cease at one moment, followed by the emergence of new formations at the subsequent moment, and if at the very next moment these too cease completely, then there cannot be any substance in these five aggregates; they are totally devoid of anything that can be taken as a truly existent "I."[14] He thus realizes the voidness of formations, which are wholly and completely devoid of the nature of a self.[15]

An experienced meditator will see how, through the gradual development of insight knowledge gained by contemplation, the defilements rooted in his mind are ceasing by way of substitution of opposites.[16] As the real nature of formations is progressively revealed by the light of insight knowledge, the darkness of ignorance disappears, overwhelmed by the luminosity of wisdom. One eliminates the false view that there is an "I," a person, within the five aggregates. Craving ceases, since one is no longer disposed to cling to formations as "I" or "mine." Conceit vanishes, as one does not apprehend an "I" to use as the criterion for judging oneself and others. Anger is relinquished, for the beings and persons with whom one normally enters into conflict are now seen to be merely congeries of formations rather than concrete individuals. One's mind is utterly purged of the perverted perception that the world of formations is permanent, pleasurable, and beautiful.

One loses one's deeply ingrained longing for the prolonged continuity of the flux of formations.

When the meditator realizes that these defilements—which have kept him tethered to the cycle of existence—cease through substitution by their opposites, he becomes convinced that for him the suffering of saṁsāra itself is also subsiding right in the present. By developing an attitude of wise equanimity towards the different aspects of suffering such as old age, disease, physical pain, and death, their tormenting nature comes to an end. One is no longer subject to the lashings of sorrow, lamentation, despair, grief, stress, frustration, and similar misfortunes. The mass of saṁsāric suffering, to which one had been subject for so long by clinging to the five aggregates, also fades away through the substitution of opposites. Stated otherwise, the meditator sees how suffering ceases when the cycle of dependent arising is terminated by nullifying the root defilements of ignorance and craving.[17]

With the perfection of the thirty-seven requisites of enlightenment (*bodhipakkhiyā dhammā*), a well-sharpened process of intense insight meditation spontaneously sets in. Then, at an unexpected but conspicuous stage of the meditative process, the contemplation of cessation reaches its consummation. As one is profoundly immersed in one of the three contemplations—of impermanence, suffering, or non-self—suddenly the object of contemplation totally ceases and, for just a moment, even while remaining extremely alert, the mind forsakes all mundane objects. Then it immediately takes up once again the subject of meditation and reverts to the contemplation of insight, experiencing great joy. What takes place in that momentary shift in consciousness is the opening of the stainless and immaculate eye of the Dhamma: "Whatever is of the nature of origination, all that is of the nature of cessation."[18] This is nothing other than the attainment of the supramundane path and fruit, which have as their object of realization Nibbāna, the ultimate cessation (*accanta-nirodha*) or emancipatory cessation (*nissaraṇa-nirodha*).[19] At this stage, by the penetration of Nibbāna as ultimate cessation, one accomplishes the extirpative cessation (*anuppāda-* or *samuccheda-nirodha*) of defilements, eradicating them so that they can never again emerge in the future.[20]

Abandoning Origination

It is said "the contemplation of cessation abandons origination." Considering the basic nature of this contemplation, the term "origination" (*samudaya*) here can be taken as conveying the idea of the origination or birth of formations,[21] for when the contemplation is confined to momentary dissolution, one stops attending to their origination. Nevertheless, when the wide area covered by the contemplation of cessation is taken into account, and when we consider that the term "origination" should signify a defilement eliminated by this contemplation, we can conclude that the "origination" here conveys a still deeper meaning. That is, it can signify the condition responsible for the repeated emergence of formations in the future, i.e. the defilements, specifically craving. This assumption becomes justifiable on the ground that the repeated observation of the cessation of formations leads to revulsion towards them and disenchantment with them, which in turn eliminates the craving for the further prolongation of this continuity of formations. As such it can be stated that, in this context, all the defilements responsible for the continued emergence of formations are comprised by the term origination (*samudaya*).[22]

The *Paṭisambhidāmagga Commentary*, while interpreting the contemplation of cessation as contemplation of the cessation of passion, explains origination as the coming into being of passion.[23] Whether passion (*rāga*) is regarded as a term representing all the defilements pertaining to origination or as one major defilement of this category, it corresponds with the interpretation of the term given above, that is, as meaning the cause for the continued arising of formations in the cycle of rebirths.

In the light of the comprehensive interpretation of the contemplation of cessation and of origination so far adduced, this contemplation becomes definable as an amalgamation of all the three contemplations of impermanence, suffering, and non-self. The *Paṭisambhidāmagga* says that all these three contemplations become operative within the knowledge of dissolution (*bhaṅga-ñāṇa*), which is an important stage in the contemplation of cessation.[24] In the same work, where the contemplations have been classified on the basis of the kind of clinging they eliminate, the contemplation of cessation again seems to be an amalgamation of all three contemplations, or at least of two of them.[25] But considering the basic nature of the contemplation of cessation, as attention to the passing away of formations, it would be better to treat it mainly as a variant of the contemplation of impermanence.

In many places where the contemplations of impermanence, of dispassion, and of cessation occur together, the commentary analyses the latter two in identical terms. It classifies dispassion as destructional dispassion (*khaya-virāga*) and as ultimate dispassion (*accanta-virāga*), while it classifies cessation as destructional cessation (*khaya-nirodha*) and as ultimate cessation (*accanta-nirodha*). Here the commentary explains that destructional dispassion and destructional cessation both refer to the momentary dissolution of formations, while ultimate dispassion and ultimate cessation both refer to Nibbāna.[26] Hence these two contemplations appear to be identical. In addition, passion and origination (of suffering), which are the two defilements respectively eliminated by these two contemplations, also display a close similarity to each other, both being synonyms for craving (*taṇhā*).

Nevertheless, the *Paṭisambhidāmagga Commentary* has attempted to indicate a distinction between these two contemplations. In explaining the schedule on mindfulness of breathing (*ānāpānasati-mātikā*), this commentary says that the contemplation of dispassion is the insight capable of generating detachment towards formations (i.e. emphasizing here dispassion through the substitution of opposites), whereas the contemplation of cessation is a more potent variety of insight capable of effecting the cessation of defilements.[27]

In its gloss on the knowledge of comprehension (*sammasana-ñāṇa*) the same commentary says that while dispassion is the total transcendence of the existing state, cessation is the complete and irreversible extinction of that state.[28] What is explained here under dispassion is the momentary destruction of phenomena (*khaya-virāga*). Considered in this light, the contemplation of cessation by way of the destruction of phenomena goes deeper than the contemplation of dispassion by way of the destruction of phenomena.

In describing insight through mindfulness of breathing, the *Paṭisambhidāmagga* includes a special analysis of the doctrine of dependent arising when recounting the contemplation of cessation but not when recounting the contemplation of dispassion. According to the commentary, this is an indication of the superiority of the former contemplation over the latter.[29]

The *Paṭisambhidāmagga Commentary* further indicates that the contemplation of cessation goes deeper than that of dispassion because the former eradicates the origin or source of passion while the latter removes passion alone.

Both ultimate dispassion and ultimate cessation, as stated earlier, refer to Nibbāna. If the contemplation of dispassion is regarded as a variant of the contemplation of suffering and the contemplation of cessation as a variant of the contemplation of impermanence, then it follows that the two contemplations become distinct doors to liberation (*vimokkha-mukha*) revealing different aspects of Nibbāna. Accordingly, ultimate dispassion turns out to be Nibbāna apprehended by way of the desireless liberation (i.e. as liberation devoid of any yearning for pleasure) at the moment when the contemplation of dispassion reaches its culmination; ultimate cessation turns out to be Nibbāna apprehended by way of the signless liberation (i.e. liberation devoid of any fixed sign of permanence in formations) at the moment when the contemplation of cessation reaches its culmination.[30]

Practically speaking, in insight meditation, dispassion is very often experienced as the fading away of passion, or as equanimity, while cessation is frequently realized as the cessation of formations occurring in diverse ways.

Mindfulness of death never leaves the meditator who seriously engages in the contemplation of cessation. Therefore he applies himself to insight meditation with increasing diligence, hoping to achieve thereby the extirpative cessation of formations.

* * *

> "Monks, through the development and cultivation of the contemplation of cessation one may expect one of two fruits: either the final knowledge of arahantship in this very life, or if any more defilements still remain, the stage of non-returner."[31]

7

Contemplation of Relinquishment (*Paṭinissaggānupassanā*)

One who develops the contemplation of relinquishment abandons grasping.

(*Paṭinissaggānupassanaṁ bhāvento ādānaṁ pajahati.*)

Two Types of Relinquishment

In the texts, two meanings have been adduced for the term *paṭinissagga*,[1] "relinquishment": (i) giving up (*pariccāga*); and (ii) entering into (*pakkhandana*).[2] The more important of the two is the idea of "giving up," which implies the sense of "abandonment" or "dropping off" (*pahāna*).[3] Accordingly, on the authority of the analysis of relinquishment in the "Mindfulness of Breathing" chapter of the *Paṭisambhidāmagga*, it can be concluded that relinquishment by way of abandonment (*pariccāga-paṭinissagga*) signifies the "dropping off" or abandoning of the totality of formations categorized diversely as the aggregates, elements, sense bases, faculties, spheres of becoming, jhānas, factors of dependent origination, etc.[4]

The following discourse of the Buddha clarifies how abandonment in the sense of giving up should be extended to the entire gamut of formations:

> "Monks, everything should be abandoned. And what is this everything that should be abandoned? The eye should be abandoned. So too visible forms, eye-consciousness, eye-contact, and whatever feeling is generated through such contact—whether pleasant, painful, or neutral—all this should be abandoned."[5]

The Buddha then applies the same formula to the ear, nose, tongue, body, and mind.

The knowledge born of contemplation removes ignorance, thereby exposing the true nature of formations. As a result, the passionate desire or craving that compels one to grasp formations as "I" and "mine" disappears by way of the substitution of opposites, paving the way for the abandonment of all formations by way of the substitution of opposites in the very present.[6]

The giving up of presently occurring formations achieved in the course of insight meditation reaches its consummation with the total and permanent relinquishment of formations via the attainment of the supramundane path. When the supramundane path is reached, all formations totally drop away as objects of cognition and the mind directly penetrates the unconditioned state, Nibbāna. Here the defilements pertaining to each path and the respective kamma they would generate, along with the aggregates that they would produce in the future, are all given up by way of extirpation. For this reason the supramundane path, too, is referred to as "relinquishment by way of giving up" (*pariccāga-paṭinissagga*).[7]

The other meaning conveyed by the term *paṭinissagga* is "entering into," "launching into," or "immersion in." It is the mind's entering into Nibbāna that is referred to as "relinquishment (of formations) through immersion."[8]

The act of "relinquishment through entering into" becomes functional in the same two stages: insight and the supramundane path. When the meditator sees the dangers inherent in formations with the knowledge of insight, his mind inclines towards Nibbāna as a state free from such dangerous formations; this is the "relinquishment through entering into" that becomes functional at the level of insight. Then, at the stage of the supramundane path, one relinquishes all formations by actually fully immersing the mind in Nibbāna;

thus the supramundane path too has been defined as "relinquishment through entering into."[9]

The repeated development of insight knowledge for the cultivation of the two aspects of relinquishment—as the giving up of formations and as entering into Nibbāna—constitutes the contemplation of relinquishment.[10]

This "giving up" and "immersion" pertaining to the contemplation of relinquishment can actually be shown as two aspects of the same attainment. Simultaneously with the abandonment of defilements and other formations the mind becomes oriented towards Nibbāna; this orientation becomes increasingly more evident in the higher stages of insight meditation. At the stage of the supramundane path both these events occur at the same instant: at the very same moment that the mind enters into Nibbāna by taking Nibbāna as its direct object, the defilements to be eradicated by that path, and the formations to be produced by those defilements, are forever abandoned. Thus it can be maintained that although relinquishment is twofold in theory, it is unitary in direct experience.

Abandonment is in fact the essence of insight meditation, underlying and embracing the entire meditative path. Relinquishment begins initially on a low key and gradually gathers momentum until it reaches such a high pitch that it gives one the enormous strength required to abandon the defilements and formations in their entirety.

The Unfolding Process of Relinquishment

The first major task of the meditator developing a subject of pure insight meditation is the elimination of the hindrances (*nīvaraṇa*): this is a giving up of defilements. Following their removal, when the meditator's mind becomes fully concentrated, the knowledge of the delimitation of mind and matter (*nāmarūpapariccheda-ñāṇa*) dawns, debilitating the habitual perception of a self. With the perfect maturation of this knowledge one realizes that all along one had been subject to a monstrous delusion: the delusion of regarding a mere bundle of mental and material phenomena as "I" and "mine." This prepares the foundation for the giving up of formations. The strong grip on formations becomes relaxed.

This is followed by the successful attainment of the knowledge regarding the discernment of conditions (*paccaya-pariggaha-ñāṇa*). Here the grasping of formations becomes still further attenuated through confirmation of the fact that there is no "I" controlling or presiding over the process of mind and matter. One discerns that the entire process of experience occurs as a continuous series of conditionally related causes and effects. This realization gives impetus to the abandonment of formations.

The contemplation of impermanence begins to develop next in sequence. As the meditator sees how the five aggregates are subject to origination and cessation, he understands that this continuum of formations cannot contain an "I." In conformity with the contemplation of impermanence, the contemplation of suffering also becomes activated. The conviction dawns: "How can these five aggregates, which are a heap of suffering, be 'I' or 'mine'? They are simply a heap of worthless rubbish that should be totally abandoned." In this manner the contemplation of non-self also becomes sharpened, resulting in the gradual erosion of the "I"-concept. The meditator becomes more and more inclined towards relinquishment.

When he cultivates the contemplation of cessation, the meditator repeatedly observes the dissolution of the five aggregates. Thereby the dangers inherent in formations become increasingly apparent to him and intensify his contemplation of revulsion. Here the habit of finding delight (*nandi*) through the conceiving of formations as "I" or "mine" ceases and the attitude of relinquishment gathers momentum. The urge to achieve freedom from all formations becomes uppermost in the meditator's mind.

In consequence, the attachment with which one had nursed the sense faculties of the eye, ear, nose, tongue, and body—affectionately holding to them as "I" and "mine"—dies off, resulting in their spontaneous abandonment. The fivefold sensual pleasures of form, sound, smell, taste, and touch, which the meditator had been enjoying with egoistic attachment, also drop off when he realizes their frightful nature. As the "I"-concept is eliminated, he witnesses the defilements that had so far been haunting his mental continuum gradually falling away—the attachments and aversions, the likes and dislikes, the expectations, views, perverted perceptions, and theories—and he becomes equanimous.

Thus the contemplation of dispassion reaches maturity. The meditator presently becomes indifferent towards every formation that impinges on his senses; he sees to it that each object of sense dissolves then and there and is abandoned. He does not entertain any hopes for the future nor any regrets about the past.[11] Serenity is achieved presently and immediately.

With his mind deeply concentrated, the meditator experiences the true nature of the triple world. With his equanimous attitude fortified, he witnesses how the all-embracing laws of impermanence, suffering, and non-self operate continuously and universally. He penetrates the fact that the entire universe is merely a process constituted by a mutually conditioned combination of forces totally devoid of any nature of a self. There is no "I" in his range of vision, no essential difference between his group of five aggregates and the external world; no divisive separation as "here" and "there," and therefore nothing between the two.[12] Duality has been obliterated—the duality of entities, of beings, of places. Everywhere and at every moment there is only uniformity: one and the same nature of things, one and the same reality.

Here, there, and everywhere this reality is *such*. That nature of things was *such* yesterday; it is *such* today; it will be *such* tomorrow.

In this way he realizes the "suchness" (*tathatā*)—the real nature of things, the true nature of phenomena—that had so long been hidden behind the delusive screen of ignorance.[13] Respectfully he bows his head to that invariable true nature of things (*avitathatā*);[14] he falls in line with it; he does not run counter to it. He does not take naturally existent phenomena as "I" or "mine," not even the thirty-seven requisites of enlightenment that have been so immensely helpful to him.[15] In the same way that a river, whose farther shore is visible, by giving up the designation "river" unites with the great ocean, whose farther shore is invisible, the meditator, by abandoning everything divisively conceived as "I" and "mine," unites with the great flow of Dhamma.

The past has been abandoned; the future has been abandoned. As for the present, he sees that mere formations occur. Even this is abandoned by penetrating it as impermanent or suffering or non-self, thereby weakening the power of the underlying tendencies (*anusaya*).[16] Now his mind, without grasping any formation as object, becomes submerged in the realization of Nibbāna, called the state of non-grasping (*anādāna*), or the relinquishment of grasping (*ādāna-paṭinissagga*), or the relinquishment of all substrata of existence (*sabb'upadhi-paṭinissagga*).[17] Simultaneously, the defilements to be eradicated by each of the supramundane paths are also totally abandoned forever. Consequently, all the formations that might have been produced by these defilements in the future are also abandoned, even while as yet unborn.

It is in this way that the contemplation of relinquishment, which functions by abandoning formations at various stages of insight meditation, reaches its consummation at the supramundane stage.

Relinquishment by way of giving up can also be explained

as the abandonment of defilements accompanied by aggregates and kamma-formations. This is the definition given in the commentaries headed by the *Visuddhimagga*.[18] When it is defined as the giving up of all formations (as was discussed earlier in this chapter), defilements, aggregates, and kammic actions too are included. However, the elimination of defilements through the substitution of opposites occurs throughout the path of insight meditation.[19] Every contemplation so far described abandons defilements of some sort. As such, the attention to the giving up of different defilements and the resulting orientation towards Nibbāna jointly also constitute a contemplation of relinquishment.[20]

As was said earlier, the abandonment of aggregates occurs concurrently with the elimination of defilements by the substitution of opposites. Also, as long as this temporary elimination of defilements persists, no new kamma is generated by the abandoned defilements. Since these kammas remain unborn, they will not be able to produce any resultant aggregates in the future. Therefore, when defilements are eliminated by the substitution-of-opposites method, the related kamma and aggregates are also said to be abandoned.[21] In other words, this is tantamount to the relinquishment of the "three rounds" (*tivaṭṭa*): the rounds of defilements, kamma, and kamma-results. If one clearly discerns by insight knowledge how these three rounds are relinquished, that too can be considered a variant of the contemplation of relinquishment.

Contemplation of relinquishment develops gradually from the initial stages of insight meditation, widening and spreading deeper as it evolves. This contemplation, which can be regarded as the cumulative outcome of the other contemplations, is extremely helpful in rendering the insight meditation fruitful. It becomes extremely powerful in the advanced stages of insight meditation, particularly in the knowledge of desire for deliverance (*muñcitukamyatā-ñāṇa*) and the knowledge of equanimity towards formations (*saṅkhār' upekkhā-ñāṇa*).[22]

Release from Grasping

The grasping eliminated through the contemplation of relinquishment can be described as the craving which clings to formations as "I" and "mine."[23] This type of egoistic grasping occurs solely because of our inherent delusion or ignorance. It prevents us from achieving freedom from saṁsāric becoming and drives us on through the cycle of existence, in which we undergo immense suffering. However, the powerful knowledge obtained by contemplation strips away the veil of ignorance. The clear light of wisdom dawns, laying bare the true nature of the world of formations. The meditator realizes that no formation possesses any essence or value; he sees that nothing is worth grasping as "I" or "mine." He understands that no such discriminations and distinctions have any validity. The flux of formations continues uninterrupted, subject to origination and cessation. The meditator becomes convinced that within this flux there cannot be an "I" or an individual essence or some everlasting core. He clearly recognizes that the notion "I" is a deceit, a mirage, an illusion, a mere product of imagination, a mockery of truth.[24]

The meditator realizes how, by making a fruitless attempt to engender and maintain an illusory "I," one takes upon oneself an immeasurable burden of suffering. Every formation grasped in terms of "I" or "mine" changes and ceases, and this results in misery. Yet, in one's blindness, one is ready to strive, repeatedly and relentlessly, to cling to these fleeting formations in order to establish some sense of personal identity. The meditator also sees how one becomes engulfed in conflagrations of suffering by grasping even excessively harmful defilements like ignorance, craving, conceit, and views in terms of "I" and "mine." He feels that the grasping of any formation whatsoever is a dreadful hazard, a mighty blunder, like embracing a massive, red-hot iron ball or a deadly serpent.

With the maturation of this direct realization, grasping itself is relinquished and the contemplation of relinquishment penetrates still more deeply. Repeated grasping of formations is suspended; holding is abandoned.

Since the abandonment of formations centres around the characteristic of non-self, the contemplation of relinquishment seems to be a variant of the contemplation of non-self. As the grasping eliminated here is based on craving, it contains an element of the contemplation of suffering as well. However, the contemplation of relinquishment can be regarded as the consummation of the three basic contemplations.[25]

A special mode of the contemplation of relinquishment is found in the Dīghanakha Sutta of the Majjhima Nikāya.[26] To Dīghanakha, the wandering ascetic, the Buddha first delivered a discourse on the abandonment of the wrong views of annihilationism, eternalism, and partial eternalism so that Dīghanakha could discard the annihilationist viewpoint that he had adopted earlier. In order to remove his attachment to the physical body, the Buddha next taught him eleven ways to contemplate the body:

> "This body, Aggivessana—which is material, made up of the four great elements, originating from parents, nourished on porridge and sour milk, subject to impermanence, to rubbing, pounding, breaking apart, and dispersal—should be regarded as impermanent, suffering, a disease, a boil, a dart, a misfortune, an affliction, as something alien, as subject to disintegration, as empty, as non-self. When he regards this body thus, whatever desire, affection, or subservience there is towards this body is eliminated."

Then the Master enumerated the three feelings—pleasant, painful, and neutral—showing that when one of these is present the other two are absent; thereby he highlighted the characteristics of impermanence and non-self. He also explained to him how revulsion (*nibbidā*), dispassion (*virāga*), and release (*vimutti*) can be realized by comprehending that all three types of feeling are impermanent, conditioned, dependently arisen, subject to destruction, falling away, fading away, and cessation. At the conclusion of the sermon Dīghanakha became a stream-enterer (*sotāpanna*).

While this discourse was being spoken, the Venerable Sāriputta listened closely while fanning the Buddha. It then occurred to him: "The Blessed One has taught us to abandon different formations by understanding them thoroughly with wisdom. The Well-farer has told us to relinquish different formations by comprehending them clearly with wisdom." While reflecting in this way, the Venerable Sāriputta's mind was released from the cankers and he became an arahant. Accordingly, it is clear that by correctly applying one's mind to the elimination or relinquishment of formations, the contemplation of relinquishment will gain momentum and culminate in the realization of arahantship.

The meditator can currently achieve much solace by relinquishing formations inclusive of defilements. By taking upon himself the deadweight of formations grasped as "I" and "mine," he has all along been a slave to defilements, blissfully ignorant of his defenceless condition. But at last he beholds the truth through insight-wisdom. When he realizes how he has been suffering pointlessly under a useless burden, he gradually throws off this oppressive load of formations. As he experiences partial relief by partial elimination of the burden, he becomes eager to rid himself, permanently and totally, of the whole burden. Eventually, he throws off the entire load, experiencing here and now great relief, peace, consolation, serenity, and coolness—a sense of freedom and bliss too deep for words.[27]

* * *

"Therefore, monks, whatever is not yours, abandon it. Abandoning it will lead to your well-being and happiness for a long time.

"And what is it, monks, that is not yours? Material form is not yours: abandon it! Abandoning it will lead to your well-being and happiness for a long time. Feeling is not yours ... Perception is not yours ... Mental formations are not yours ... Consciousness is not yours: abandon it! Abandoning it will lead to your well-being and happiness for a long time."[28]

8

Synopsis

In the preceding chapters we have discussed the seven contemplations of insight individually, only occasionally throwing sidelong glances at their interconnections. Let us now consider the seven contemplations as a whole.

The *Paṭisambhidāmagga* defines the functional nature of the seven contemplations of insight as follows:

> One repeatedly sees in terms of impermanence, not in terms of permanence. One repeatedly sees in terms of suffering, not in terms of happiness. One repeatedly sees in terms of non-self, not in terms of self. One develops revulsion; one does not find delight. One becomes dispassionate; one does not become attached. One brings to cessation; one does not originate. One relinquishes; one does not grasp.
>
> Seeing repeatedly in terms of impermanence, one abandons the perception of permanence. Seeing repeatedly in terms of suffering, one abandons the perception of happiness. Seeing repeatedly in terms of non-self, one abandons the perception of self. Becoming repelled, one abandons delight. Not attaching oneself, one abandons passion. Bringing to cessation, one abandons origination. Relinquishing, one abandons grasping.[1]

This passage demonstrates that among the seven contemplations, the contemplations of impermanence, suffering, and non-self form the nucleus, serving as the foundation for the remaining four. The *Paṭisambhidāmagga* refers to the first three as contemplations (*anupassanā*) and to the other four as insights (*vipassanā*).[2] In actuality, it is the variations of these three primary contemplations that function throughout insight meditation.

Further, a methodical relationship among the seven contemplations is displayed here. The relationships among the three basic contemplations were discussed in earlier chapters. Generally, the contemplation of impermanence entails contemplation of suffering, while both entail the contemplation of non-self. These three contemplations generate revulsion, the contemplation of which produces dispassion. The contemplation of dispassion brings cessation; the contemplation of cessation, relinquishment.

In theory the path of insight contemplation can be elucidated entirely by this method. In living experience, however, insight does not invariably unfold in this order. The development of insight is a complex process in which any contemplation may condition the others in a wide variety of ways. In one passage the *Paṭisambhidāmagga* itself shows how cessation (*nirodha*) occurs subsequent to relinquishment (*paṭinissagga*).[3] Further, either the contemplation of cessation as the momentary destruction of phenomena, or of dispassion as the momentary destruction of phenomena, can be responsible for the generation and activation of the remaining contemplations. Also, the supramundane path, which is the consummation of insight, can be presented as any one from among the contemplations of dispassion, cessation, and relinquishment.

In the delineation of the contemplations we have seen how one and the same contemplation can come to the fore at different stages along the path of insight. With the gradual maturation of insight the contemplation becomes correspondingly deeper and wider, while the resulting realization and the abandonment of defilements also become correspondingly sharper. Accordingly, there is no hard and fast rule that one contemplation has to reach its zenith before the next in the series can begin. The contemplations are characterized by a gradual evolution and reciprocal influence. But at certain junctures along the path of insight a particular contemplation may become especially prominent. At other times several contemplations may function alternately. Also the same contemplation will surface in different forms under different conditions.

It appears that certain contemplations bear close resemblances to one another. Looking at the matter from a practical point of view, it is difficult to decide to which contemplation certain stages of insight should be assigned. But this should not be a burden to the meditator. If mindfulness and clear comprehension are correctly applied, suitable contemplations will arise and develop almost effortlessly. It is not necessary for one to be concerned with labelling the particular type of contemplation in which one is engaged while practising insight. Even if such a conviction emerges spontaneously, one should incorporate that too into the development of insight by contemplating it as a mere formation.

When one considers the variations in the individual aptitudes of people, it is difficult to present a common programme of contemplation suitable for everyone. But it can be stated that for any meditator who progresses along the path of insight systematically and correctly, all these seven contemplations will develop. It appears that in this context the meditator's prior experiences in insight meditation in past lives play a major role.

However, if there are interruptions and retrogressions in the insight meditation, or if mental hindrances (*nīvaraṇa*) emerge intermittently, it is advisable to pay greater attention to a contemplation befitting the context. For example, a certain meditator, confronted with an onset of violent passion, developed the contemplation of dispassion. His attention then gradually assumed depth, culminating in the total abandonment of passion, so that even by effort he could not generate a passionate thought!

The *Paṭisambhidāmagga* states that the seven contemplations (as they were shown at the beginning of this chapter) become functional within the knowledge of dissolution (*bhaṅga-ñāṇa*),[4] which confirms that this knowledge has a wide diffusion. Accordingly, the *Visuddhimagga* says that the seven contemplations become predominant at the third stage of the path of insight, known as the full understanding of abandonment (*pahāna-pariññā*), which extends from the knowledge of dissolution upwards.[5]

This, however, does not imply that these contemplations do not become active prior to the stage of the knowledge of dissolution. This fact is clearly stated in the *Visuddhimagga* itself.[6] By introducing the path of insight entirely through the eighteen principal insights headed by the seven contemplations, even the *Paṭisambhidāmagga* indicates in several places that these contemplations become functional starting from the initial stages of insight meditation.[7] But it can be said that it is from the knowledge of dissolution onwards that the contemplations acquire formidable power in eliminating the defilements on a major scale. The knowledge of dissolution is thus an important juncture in the path of insight. If treated as a contemplation, the knowledge of dissolution can be classified either as the contemplation of cessation (considered as the momentary cessation of formations) or as the contemplation of dispassion (considered as the momentary destruction of formations).

In the *Paṭisambhidāmagga* the four foundations of mindfulness—mindfulness of the body, feelings, mind, and mind-objects—are also defined as contemplations to be practised on the basis of the seven contemplations.[8] Likewise, the same treatise explains how to practise insight through the seven contemplations at each of the sixteen steps in meditation on mindfulness of breathing.[9]

The seven contemplations have been designated as "insight powers" (*vipassanā-bala*) in the sense that they cannot be shaken by the defilements that they relinquish.[10] This condition becomes a basis for the attainment of cessation (*nirodha-samāpatti*) as well.[11] In the presentation of various other definitions, too, the *Paṭisambhidāmagga* refers to the seven contemplations and the defilements eliminated by them.[12]

But apart from the *Paṭisambhidāmagga*, there is no other text in the Sutta Piṭaka in which the seven contemplations and the defilements eliminated by them are presented in this manner. Although some of the Buddha's discourses mention one or several of these seven contemplations by name,[13] we have not come across a single discourse in which all seven are enumerated together.

In certain discourses the Buddha designates these contemplations as "perceptions" (*saññā*).[14] These, along with their counterparts among the contemplations, are as follows:

1. Perception of impermanence = contemplation of impermanence.
2. Perception of suffering = contemplation of suffering.
3. Perception of non-self = contemplation of non-self.
4. Perception of distaste for the whole world = contemplation of revulsion.
5. Perception of dispassion = contemplation of dispassion.
6. Perception of cessation = contemplation of cessation.
7. Perception of abandonment = contemplation of relinquishment.

In certain contexts these seven perceptions are found preceded by three other perceptions pertaining to serenity meditation (*samatha-saññā*).[15] Of course, many discourses make mention of these perceptions either individually or in smaller groups.[16]

Several discourses contain the expression "perception of impermanence in all formations" (*sabbasaṅkhāresu aniccasaññā*). The way it is explained here gives the impression that this refers to revulsion or dispassion.[17]

In many discourses the Buddha demonstrates how revulsion (*nibbidā*) and dispassion (*virāga*) are generated following the three contemplations of impermanence, suffering, and non-self (most of the passages cited in Chapter 4 are of this type). There are also discourses in which the three terms—revulsion, dispassion, and cessation—occur consecutively.[18]

Another method of contemplation commonly occurring in the texts involves examining the five aggregates and other formations thus: "It is impermanent, conditioned, dependently arisen, subject to destruction, subject to fall, subject to dispassion, subject to cessation."[19] In this technique the characteristic of impermanence takes precedence. "Destruction" and "fall" (*khaya* and *vaya*) here represent the contemplation of cessation, though among the eighteen principal insights these are enumerated in their own right as separate contemplations (see Appendix 5). "Dispassion" might refer to the momentary destruction of phenomena (*khaya-virāga*) or to dispassion as detachment occurring through the substitution of opposites. Both the terms "conditioned" (*saṅkhata*) and "dependently arisen" (*paṭicca-samuppanna*) indicate impermanence as well as the nature of non-self.

In certain discourses dealing with the elimination of defilements, the terms destruction (*khaya*), dispassion (*virāga*), cessation (*nirodha*), giving up (*cāga*), and relinquishment (*paṭinissagga*) occur consecutively.[20] Here "giving up" (*cāga*) is synonymous with relinquishment (*paṭinissagga*) itself.

There are other methods of contemplation expounded in diverse ways without overt reference to the seven contemplations. In the *Paṭisambhidāmagga* we find a collection of special terms expressive of contemplations of this category. This collection consists of forty terms including impermanence, suffering, and non-self. The text further distributes these forty terms among the three contemplations of impermanence, suffering, and non-self.[21] Although no single discourse of the Buddha is found mentioning all these forty methods of contemplation together, many discourses cite eleven or fewer of them.[22] The *Visuddhimagga* too employs these forty contemplations for elucidating several stages of the path of insight.[23]

It was stated at the very outset that the seven contemplations constitute the basic segment of the eighteen principal insights. Even the other great contemplations of this series represent diversified expressions of this basic segment of seven.[24]

The analysis of the seven contemplations is hereby concluded. This series of seven contemplations is indeed a flight of steps leading infallibly to Nibbāna.

* * *

> The contemplation of impermanence, when developed and cultivated, fulfils swift wisdom.
>
> The contemplation of suffering, when developed and cultivated, fulfils discriminating wisdom.
>
> The contemplation of non-self, when developed and cultivated, fulfils great wisdom.
>
> The contemplation of revulsion, when developed and cultivated, fulfils sharp wisdom.
>
> The contemplation of dispassion, when developed and cultivated, fulfils extensive wisdom.
>
> The contemplation of cessation, when developed and cultivated, fulfils deep wisdom.
>
> The contemplation of relinquishment, when developed and cultivated, fulfils unapproachable wisdom.
>
> By developing and cultivating these seven contemplations, there comes fulfilment of sagacious wisdom [characterized by the knowledges of equanimity towards formations, of conformity with truth, and of change-of-lineage].
>
> By developing and cultivating these eight forms of wisdom, there comes the fulfilment of diversified wide wisdom [characterized by the knowledge of path and fruit].

By developing and cultivating these nine forms of wisdom, there comes the fulfilment of delightful wisdom [designated reviewing knowledge].[25]

Postscript

So far we have been offering a few pointers in the path to the overcoming of sorrow and the realization of genuine happiness. It is the responsibility of each individual to develop this path and to realize that happiness. Therefore let all those who are endowed with confidence and wisdom be diligent in making full use of this rare opportunity of being born as human beings at the correct time, obtained through previous merit.

* * *

> "Monks, whatever should be done by a sincere and compassionate teacher out of compassion for the well-being of his disciples, that has been done by me for you. These are the roots of trees, these are empty places. Meditate, monks, do not be negligent, lest you be remorseful later. This is our admonition to you."[26]

Appendix 1

Conventional and Ultimate Truth

Truth is twofold: conventional truth (*sammuti-sacca*) and ultimate truth (*paramattha-sacca*). There are certain situations and objects that are true by usage, as they seem to be true by ordinary criteria and they make communication easier. These are accordingly designated conventional truths or conventional realities. When these conventional realities are analysed with wisdom, we find that they do not exist in the way they are conceived. While they are conceived to be real, substantial entities, in actuality they are mere conceptual constructs superimposed upon truly existent phenomena. Those things that are truly existent are called ultimate truths or ultimate realities.

Consider your own personality. You make use of the expression "I." Such commonplace phrases as "I go," "I experience," "I recognize," "I act," "I know," etc., convey the impression that there is a real independent "I" within oneself. But if this entity called "I" is investigated to discover its real identity, all we find is a combination of the five aggregates—material form, feeling, perception, mental formations, and consciousness—which are further bifurcated as mind and matter. Among all these phenomena of existence, what is it that can be taken as a real "I"? If the physical body is analysed further into the thirty-two parts—head hairs, body hairs, nails, teeth, skin, flesh, sinews, bones, etc.—the conventional notion of "I" collapses. When these material phenomena are analysed still further with wisdom, it will be seen that they are all composed of the basic elements: the hard-soft, coarse nature (= the earth element; *paṭhavi-dhātu*); the cohesive-fluid, adhesive nature (= the water element; *āpo-dhātu*); the hot-cold, digestive nature (= the fire element; *tejo-dhātu*); the supportive-mobile, expanding nature (= the air element; *vāyo-dhātu*); and the void, empty nature (= the space element; *ākāsa-dhātu*).

The mind is also a mere form of energy capable of cognizing objects; thus it too is classified as an element, namely, "the element of consciousness" (*viññāṇa-dhātu*). Accordingly, although "I" is accepted as an actuality at the level of convention, there is no "I" in the ultimate sense. What is found in reality is a compound of six elements devoid of any nature of a being or an individual.

In reality what is diffused throughout the entire universe is only these six elements of solidity, fluidity, heat, motion, space, and consciousness. These are not substances, but mere forms of energy continuously changing on the basis of a cause-and-effect relationship. They are merely continuities of dynamic processes originating and ceasing so quickly that their tranformations cannot be perceived by ordinary means.

All entities that are supposed to exist—whether conscious or without consciousness—are merely diverse combinations of these elements. They can be regarded as real only within the limits of convention; the same applies to the designations accepted for their identification. Accordingly, terms such as sea, mountain, tree, land, house, bed, chair, clothes, people, gods, animals, "I," and "you" along with the things they denote, are all mere concepts (*paññatti*) or conventions (*sammuti*). When words themselves are mere conventions, it follows that the terms identifying ultimate realities are also mere conventions. Still, whatever conventional terms are used to designate them, their nature as ultimate realities remains unaffected.

Within and around us, the ultimate realities are in operation all the time, but we do not see this truth because of our delusion—which too is an ultimate reality pertaining to the element of consciousness, namely, *avijjā* or ignorance. By accepting convention itself as the ultimate truth, we accumulate more and more suffering.

The technique prescribed for removing this veil of ignorance and bringing to light the ultimate truth is insight meditation. Insight meditation begins with a conventional reality as object, such as mindfulness of breathing, the thirty-two constituents of the body, or the rise and fall of the abdomen. As the meditator's mindfulness and awareness deepen, he will surpass the conventional level and directly discern the ultimate realities. By repeatedly contemplating these ultimate realities from various angles the meditator gains insight into the true nature of the conditioned world. Through this insight he eradicates attachment to the world and realizes the supramundane ultimate reality, Nibbāna, thereby gaining release from suffering.

The mundane ultimate realities, recounted here as the six elements, have to be comprehended as they really are through personal experience. Nevertheless, up to a certain point they can also be verbally described, though inadequately. In contrast, the supramundane ultimate reality, Nibbāna, resists all attempts at verbal description, for it is beyond all mundane standards, conventions, and designations such as space and time. Nibbāna, however, can be directly perceived by intuitive wisdom, which arises by fulfilling the path to enlightenment.

In our day to day activities we have to resort to convention, but it is good to remember that it is not the ultimate truth.

Appendix 2

Two Kinds of Knowledge

Erudition acquired by studying the Dhamma is theoretical knowledge, knowledge based on "hearing" or learning (*sutamaya-ñāṇa*). This type of knowledge is confined to the conventional level. Direct personal understanding of the Dhamma gained through insight meditation is experiential knowledge, knowledge based on meditation (*bhāvanāmaya-ñāṇa*).

Extensive learning is not critically necessary for a meditator who resides with an experienced meditation master and practises under his personal guidance. This is because he receives the necessary instructions from the teacher systematically at the appropriate times. A person who practises meditation without such personal guidance will require a very clear theoretical knowledge about the path of meditation. Stories about some of the early monks who practised on their own reveal that at the very outset they had acquired from their teachers sufficient theoretical knowledge about the way of practice right up to arahantship. It was only after they had mastered such knowledge that they resorted to seclusion in order to practise what they had learnt. It appears that in the *Visuddhimagga* and the commentaries a method of mental development has been indicated whereby knowledge based on meditation can be generated solely through the guidance of knowledge based on learning. The schedule on knowledge (*ñāṇa-mātikā*) in the *Paṭisambhidāmagga*, too, emphasizes knowledge based on learning.

Knowledge based on learning can sometimes become an obstruction to meditation. The meditator who knows the different stages in the path of practice may wait expectantly for them to arise. At times he may even delude himself into thinking he has reached them. If the meditation develops properly, he becomes exultant and clings to his experiences, gives rise to conceit, or adopts a wrong view; if it does not develop properly, he becomes dejected and disappointed. If such situations are not overcome promptly either through one's own intelligent examination or through the advice of a teacher, the meditation will degenerate.

Therefore the meditator endowed with theoretical knowledge should always recognize the primacy of the knowledge based on meditation. Although theoretical knowledge is useful as an aid for generating the knowledge based on meditation, one should be cautious not to identify the two.

Theoretical knowledge can be employed to eliminate certain impediments on the path of meditation. For instance, the meditator who is aware of the "corruptions of insight" (*vipassan'upakkilesa*), which may set in during the initial stage of the knowledge of rise and fall, might find such knowledge helpful in overcoming them. Likewise, theoretical knowledge can help to identify in conventional terms the realizations achieved in meditation. When one realizes the nature of the earth element through meditational knowledge, the identification of it as "the earth element" follows only if one has proper theoretical knowledge. Yet the progress of meditation does not depend on the ability to comprehend in conventional terms the diverse realizations attained through the practice. This is because insight meditation, being aimed at the penetration of the ultimate realities, supersedes the level of conventional realities. Preoccupation with conventional terms can actually be an obstacle to meditation. There is no harm if the juxtaposition of meditational experiences with conventional concepts occurs spontaneously. But otherwise, contemplation should be continued without dallying with conceptual interpretations.

The realization of truth can be consummated only through meditational knowledge. Only a partial mastery of truth can be achieved through knowledge based on learning and on reasoning. Therefore, without becoming complacent over one's scholastic proficiency and powers of reasoning, one should make every effort to attain direct knowledge, which is possible only through insight meditation.

Appendix 3

The Four Protective Meditations

Four subjects of meditation can help the novice meditator to stabilize his mind: meditation on the virtues of the Buddha, meditation on loving-kindness, meditation on foulness, and mindfulness of death. These four are also known as "the four protective meditations" (*caturārakkhā-bhāvanā*) on account of the nourishment and protection they afford in diverse ways to the basic meditation practice.

By meditating on the virtues of the Buddha (*buddhaguṇa-bhāvanā* or *buddhānussati*) strong confidence in the Master is established. This serves as a basis for generating the courage required to pursue the meditation unobstructed. It will increase zest and make the mind serene, thereby creating the mental framework appropriate for meditation.

Meditation on loving-kindness (*mettā-bhāvanā*) makes the mind supple. It subdues anger, which is a powerful impediment to meditation. It enables one to continue the meditation happily, unobstructed, overcoming all impediments. It allows one to develop concentration up to the third jhāna.

Meditation on foulness (*asubha-bhāvanā* or *kāyagatāsati*) removes sensual desire, a major hindrance to concentration. By casting out all undue expectations regarding one's physical body and enabling one to endure the physical suffering, it makes one's mind quite amenable to meditation. Through this meditation the first jhāna can be attained as well as insight.

By developing mindfulness of death (*maraṇasati*), intoxication with life is removed. Fear of saṁsāra is increased. A vigorous attempt is made to consummate the meditation. One becomes more adept in applying oneself to insight meditation.

A mind that has achieved some degree of proficiency in these four subjects becomes properly equipped for cultivating any of the fundamental meditation subjects. Until the mind attains to full concentration through the fundamental meditation subject, it is advisable, at least at the beginning of the day's initial meditation session, to first settle the mind by developing briefly one round of these four subjects of meditation. One need not practise all four; it would be sufficient to attend to one or two that foster the required level of concentration. When this has been achieved, one may then direct attention to the fundamental meditation subject.

In cultivating these four subjects of meditation, if the meditator finds that he can develop any one of them with ease, he can utilize that particular meditation subject itself to perfect his concentration and thereby make it a basis for insight. It is even possible that insight might emerge on its own through these subjects of meditation. In such a situation it is advisable to take the cue and resort to insight.

There is another way in which the cultivation of these subjects of meditation will prove to be purposeful. Let us suppose that when a fundamental meditation subject is being developed, one of the hindrances erupts and impedes the practice. In such a situation one should suspend the fundamental meditation subject, take up instead whichever of the four protective meditation subjects fits the context, and use it to suppress the defilement. Then one can return to the fundamental meditation subject and develop it with ease.

To be specific: When one is beset by dislike, doubt, or perplexity regarding the meditation, one should recollect the Buddha's virtues. When strong anger or fear arises, one should meditate on loving-kindness. If strong lust arises, one should contemplate the foulness of the body. For indolence and despondency, one should reflect on death or on the Buddha's virtues. If the mind becomes distracted or bored, one should meditate on the Buddha's virtues or on loving-kindness.

Appendix 4

Personality View

The five aggregates, tenaciously clung to, are designated "personality" (*sakkāya*).[1] Here clinging signifies lustful desire (*chandarāga*) or craving (*taṇhā*).[2] When the five aggregates are clung to strongly with craving, they are mistakenly conceived to be a self or the belongings of a self. The outcome is what is called personality view (*sakkāya-diṭṭhi*). This personality view can occur in four modes in relation to each aggregate, making a total of twenty such modes.[3] These modes, found in the oldest suttas, are explained in detail in the *Paṭisambhidāmagga*.[4] Let us discuss them succinctly.

The Twenty Modes of Personality View

(i) *Views of Self based on Form*

1. One regards material form as the self (*rūpaṁ attato samanupassati*): The first type of personality view based on material form is obtained by conceiving the five sense faculties such as the eye, etc., the thirty-two constituents of the body beginning with head-hairs, and the counterpart signs, etc., obtained in *kasiṇa* meditation, in terms of "I" and "self." The holder of this view contends that "just as the burning flame of an oil-lamp is not different from its colour but identical with it, even so, material form and the self are not different but identical."

2. One regards the self as the possessor of material form (*rūpavantaṁ attānaṁ samanupassati*): Here the non-material constituents (*nāma*) are identified with the self. These are the four aggregates of feeling, perception, mental formations, and consciousness: "This non-material self ('I') is one thing, material form is another. As such the self ('I') is the owner of

material form." This is the second personality view based on material form. The illustration cited for this is a tree in relation to its shadow: although the tree and its shadow are different from each other, the tree is said *to have* a shadow.

3. One regards material form as in the self (*attani rūpaṁ samanupassati*): In this view too the concept of self is maintained in relation to the four non-material aggregates. After deciding that material form is in the non-material self on the basis of the existence of material form in association with the mind, the holder of this view maintains: "Material form is one thing, the non-material self is another; that material form exists in this self." He then cites an illustration: "In a fragrant flower the fragrance is one thing, the flower is another; the fragrance exists in the flower. In like manner, material form exists in the non-material self."

4. One regards the self as in material form (*rūpasmiṁ attānaṁ samanupassati*): The holder of this view conceives the four non-material aggregates to be the self and imagines this self to be existent in material form. He maintains: "This is material form; this is the self; this self exists in this material form." He then cites the illustration: "There is a gem in a casket: the casket is different from the gem; the gem is in the casket. In like manner, the self is in material form."

(ii) *Views of Self based on Feeling*

5. Identification of feeling (*vedanā*) with self. The feeling experienced through the six senses—or the three feelings of pleasure, pain, and neutral feeling—are identified with self: this is the first personality view related to feeling. It resembles the first personality view conceived on the basis of material form, discussed above.

6. Identification of self as the possessor of feeling.

7. Identification of feeling as in self.

8. Identification of self as in feeling.

In these three views, the self conceived consists of the four aggregates—material form, perception, mental formations, and consciousness—and feeling is posited in relation to this self. These views resemble the three corresponding views based on material form, explained above.

(iii) *Views of Self based on Perception*

9. Identification of perception (*saññā*) as self. It is the six perceptions pertaining to the six sense faculties that are here conceived as self. This resembles the first personality view based on material form.

10. Identification of self as the possessor of perception.

11. Identification of perception as in self.

12. Identification of self as in perception.

In the above three cases the aggregates of material form, feeling, mental formations, and consciousness are collectively treated as self. These resemble the corresponding views based on material form.

(iv) *Views of Self based on Mental Formations*

13. Identification of mental formations (*saṅkhārā*) as self. In this first personality view based on mental formations it is volition (*cetanā*) that is mainly conceived as self. It too can be considered as sixfold by relating it to the six sense faculties. It is also possible to conceive as self any of the other mental factors coming under the heading of mental formations. This resembles the first personality view based on material form.

14. Identification of self as the possessor of mental formations.

15. Identification of mental formations as in self.

16. Identification of self as in mental formations.

In the above three cases it is the aggregates of material form, feeling, perception, and consciousness that are collectively treated as the self. These resemble the corresponding views based on material form.

(v) ***Views of Self based on Consciousness***

17. Identification of consciousness (*viññāṇa*) as self. In this first view, consciousness itself, which has been classified in diverse ways, is conceived as the self. It is the counterpart of the first view based on material form.

18. Identification of self as the possessor of consciousness.

19. Identification of consciousness as in self.

20. Identification of self as in consciousness.

In these three views, material form, feeling, perception, and mental formations are collectively conceived as the self. They resemble the corresponding views based on material form.

The Fetter of Views

Although the Buddha has analysed personality view in relation to all the five aggregates, the unenlightened worldling becomes enslaved by this view owing to his inability to understand this analysis. While some conceive all the five aggregates as self, others conceive one or several of them as self, as shown above. Personality view, which is also referred to as "clinging to a doctrine of self" (*attavād'upādāna*), is more difficult to comprehend than the other three forms of clinging;[5] it is the most subtle manifestation of the underlying tendency to views (*diṭṭh'anusaya*). So long as this tendency has not been extirpated, the ignorant worldling dwells with his mind oppressed by personality view and does not know how to eliminate it.[6] Personality view thereby becomes strengthened and turns into a fetter binding the worldling to saṁsāra, the cycle of birth and death. Being ignorant of the good Dhamma, he is born in bondage, grows old in bondage, and dies in bondage; he also goes to the next birth in bondage.[7] Like a dog tethered to a post or a pole with an iron chain, he runs round and round the five aggregates; he rolls on following the aggregates; he cannot free himself from the aggregates, and thus he is not free from birth, decay, and death, from sorrow, lamentation, physical pain, mental stress, and despair.[8]

It is on account of personality view that people adopt the two extremist views of annihilationism and eternalism. If a self is admitted it must be destined either to annihilation or to eternal existence. The *Paṭisambhidāmagga* states that the five personality views which treat each aggregate individually as self (nos. 1, 5, 9, 13, and 17 above) are based on annihilationism, while the other fifteen views are based on eternalism.[9]

As the fetter of personality view along with the underlying tendency to views is totally eradicated at the stage of stream-entry,[10] the noble disciple does not entertain personality view. When he personally realizes the characteristic of non-self in the course of insight meditation, the insight meditator eliminates personality view tentatively by way of the substitution of opposites (*tadaṅga-pahāna*). The commentaries maintain that this temporary elimination occurs by perfecting the knowledge delimiting mentality and materiality (*nāmarūpapariccheda-ñāṇa*).[11] The wise worldling who has acquired a definite ascertainment regarding the nature of non-self through the study of the Dhamma may also be able to curb the active stage of personality view.

Appendix 5

The Eighteen Principal Insights

The seven contemplations of insight appear as the first seven members of a list of eighteen principal insights (*aṭṭhārasa mahāvipassanā*). A fairly thorough analysis of the seven contemplations has just been provided. Now we intend to offer a brief description of the remaining eleven insights, comparing the different ways they have been characterized by the great expositors of the Dhamma in the Theravāda tradition.

The *Paṭisambhidāmagga* is the only work in the Tipiṭaka to mention all eighteen insights, but it does not elaborate on them. It is in the *Visuddhimagga* that we find the first analytical discussion of all the eighteen insights collectively.[12] Here it is stated that these insights develop in a way appropriate to the different stages of insight meditation. But a later work, the commentary to the *Paṭisambhidāmagga,* maintains that the path of insight is accomplished gradually with all the contemplations linking up sequentially like a flight of stairs.[13] This commentarial manner of presenting the insights in sequence is based on the "Discussion of Faculties" chapter (*Indriyakathā*) in the *Paṭisambhidāmagga,* which introduces just such a sequence.[14]

Consequently, these two important works—the *Visuddhimagga* and the *Paṭisambhidāmagga Commentary*—show distinct differences in their interpretation of certain contemplations. In what follows we will indicate such differences whenever they occur, referring to the two methods of explanation separately as "Vism. Exp." and as "PmA. Exp." The former will draw upon both the *Visuddhimagga* itself and its commentary, the *Visuddhimagga Mahāṭīkā* (VismṬ.), also known as the *Paramatthamañjūsā.*

* * *

8. "One who develops the contemplation of destruction abandons the perception of compactness" (*khayānupassanaṁ bhāvento ghanasaññaṁ pajahati*).

Vism. Exp. (XXII,114): "Contemplation of destruction, however, is the knowledge in one who effects the resolution of the compact and so sees destruction as 'impermanent in the sense of destruction.'"

PmA. Exp. (74): "The contemplation of destruction is seeing the destruction of the existent aggregates immediately followed by seeing the destruction of the very mind and mental factors that perceived those aggregates."

The disintegration of the compactness in continuity (*santati-ghana*) first occurs at the levels of the knowledge of comprehension (*sammasana-ñāṇa*) and the knowledge of rise and fall (*udayabbaya-ñāṇa*). The observation that "it is impermanent in the sense of destruction" pertains to the knowledge of comprehension (Pm.i,53). Accordingly, PmA., disagreeing with the explanation provided by Vism., analyses the contemplation of destruction under the stage of the knowledge of dissolution (*bhaṅga-ñāṇa*). VismṬ., too, while approving of the explanation given in Vism., at one point states that the contemplation of destruction means contemplation of the momentary dissolution of formations (ii,417).

However, in terms of the seven contemplations, this contemplation would be a constitutent either of the contemplation of impermanence or that of cessation.

Although PmA. says that the perception of compactness means the conception of a continuity as a compact entity, the sub-commentaries state that this perception refers to four categories of compactness: compactness of continuity (*santati-ghana*), compactness of assemblage (*samūha-ghana*), compactness of functions (*kicca-ghana*), and compactness of objects (*ārammaṇa-ghana*).[15] As the contemplation of destruction is a meditation on impermanence, the PmA. interpretation seems acceptable.

9. "One who develops the contemplation of fall abandons the accumulation of formations (or of kamma)" (*vayānupassanaṁ bhāvento āyūhanaṁ pajahati*).

The contemplation of fall is defined as intentness on cessation, i.e. on dissolution, after seeing the dissolution of present formations by personal experience and of past and future formations by inference.[16] It appears that in presenting this exegesis Vism. utilized the following stanza occurring in the Pm. chapter on the knowledge of dissolution (*bhaṅga-ñāṇa*):

Ārammaṇaṁ anvayena ubho ekavavatthanā
Nirodhe adhimuttatā vayalakkhaṇā vipassanā.

"Defining both to be alike
By inference from that same object,
Intentness on cessation—these
Are insight in the mark of fall."

Accordingly, the contemplation of fall too is a constituent of either the contemplation of impermanence or of cessation.

10. "One who develops the contemplation of change abandons the perception of stability" (*vipariṇāmānupassanaṁ bhāvento dhuvasaññaṁ pajahati*).

Vism. Exp.: "The contemplation of change is seeing the twofold change in whatever has arisen, i.e. through decay and death, or it is seeing the change-over of each state determined by way of the material septad, etc."[17]

PmA. Exp.: "The contemplation of change is the knowledge which sees the changing nature of all formations pertaining to the three times—past, present, and future—as one is totally occupied with their dissolution."

Here Vism. highlights the knowledge of comprehension, while PmA. highlights the knowledge of dissolution. The contemplation of change is yet another aspect of the contemplation of impermanence.

11. "One who develops the contemplation of the signless abandons the sign" (*animittānupassanaṁ bhāvento nimittaṁ pajahati*).

The meditator who repeatedly observes that formations are devoid of permanent "signs" or attributes abandons the habit of perceiving formations unitarily as endowed with permanent signs. Here "sign" (*nimitta*) means the gross nature involved in perceiving a continuity of formations as a permanent and compact whole. The contemplation of the signless is an aspect of the contemplation of impermanence (Vism. XX,91).

12. "One who develops the contemplation of the desireless abandons desire" (*appaṇihitānupassanaṁ bhāvento paṇidhiṁ pajahati*).

One who repeatedly develops the observation of the absence of anything desirable in formations abandons the longing or craving bound up with formations. This is an aspect of the contemplation of suffering (Vism. XX,91).

13. "One who develops the contemplation of voidness abandons adherence" (*suññatānupassanaṁ bhāvento abhinivesaṁ pajahati*).

One who contemplates the voidness of selfhood in formations abandons adherence to the view of self. This is an aspect of the contemplation of non-self.[18]

14. "One who develops the 'insight into phenomena that is higher wisdom' abandons adherence to the grasping after substance" (*adhipaññā-dhammavipassanaṁ bhāvento sārādānābhinivesaṁ pajahati*).

On the interpretation of this contemplation, Vism. itself offers different explanations in different chapters:

(i) XX,91: "The 'insight into phenomena that is higher wisdom' embraces all forms of insight meditation."

(ii) XXII,118: "The 'insight into phenomena that is higher wisdom' is the insight into voidness, through dissolution, occurring thus: 'Only formations disintegrate; it is the death of formations that takes place; there is nothing more.' This insight results from seeing the disintegration both of the object and the mind that apprehended that object."

PmA. approves the second characterization given above. This definition seems to be based on a stanza cited in the chapter on knowledge of dissolution, where we find the phrase "insight that is higher wisdom" (*adhipaññā-vipassanā*).[19] The full expression "insight into phenomena that is higher wisdom" (*adhipaññā-dhammavipassanā*) occurs in several discourses of the Aṅguttara Nikāya, where it bears a wide sense comprising all three stages of the path of insight meditation: seeing (*daṭṭhabba*), comprehension (*sammasitabba*), and insight proper (*vipassitabba*).[20] This hypothesis is further confirmed by the statement in the *Puggalapaññatti* asserting that the person endowed with the insight into phenomena that is higher wisdom is a winner of the paths and fruits.[21] The phrase *adhipaññā-dhammavipassanā*, then, does not denote a particular stage or aspect of insight but is a general term for true insight itself. Accordingly, the first definition of Vism. above is more appropriate, in which case it becomes rather difficult to take the phrase *adhipaññā-dhammavipassanā* as referring to a single contemplation. We should further note that unlike the names of the other contemplations in this series, this designation does not end in *-anupassanā*.

15. "One who develops the correct knowledge and vision abandons adherence to bewilderment" (*yathābhūtañāṇadassanaṁ bhāvento sammohābhinivesaṁ pajahati*).

This means that the person who develops insight into the real nature of formations gives up the tendency to become confused about the nature of formations.

Vism. Exp.: "Correct knowledge and vision is the comprehension of mind and matter along with their causes and conditions, i.e. the knowledge of delimitation of mind and matter and of the discernment of conditions" (Vism. XXII,119).

PmA. Exp.: "Correct knowledge and vision is the knowledge of appearance as terror; this is the realization that formations are fraught with terror, which results from seeing their dissolution."

As these two statements refer to different stages of insight, we have to resort to the Buddha's own words to discover what is really meant by "correct knowledge and vision" (*yathābhūta-ñāṇadassana*). In a number of discourses the Buddha recommends an unfailing method for developing dispassion by means of revulsion.[22] The latter results from correct knowledge and vision, which in turn arises from concentration. From this it is clear that correct knowledge and vision pervades the entire process of insight meditation from its starting point through to the knowledge of revulsion or the mature contemplation of revulsion. In this regard the Saṁyutta Commentary says that "correct knowledge and vision" extends from the knowledge of delimitation of mind and matter up to the knowledge of what is path and non-path (i.e. the mature knowledge of rise and fall), while "revulsion" extends from the knowledge of appearance as terror up to the knowledge of equanimity regarding formations.[23] In several places the commentaries to the above-mentioned discourses state that "correct knowledge and vision" is initial insight (*taruṇa-vipassanā*), while "revulsion" is mature insight (*balava-vipassanā*).[24] Hence it is obvious that "correct knowledge and vision" does not represent a single contemplation but is a phrase designating a particular stage comprising a number of contemplations along the path of insight meditation. Here too the designation *yathābhūta-ñāṇadassana* does not terminate in *-anupassanā*. Since "correct knowledge and vision" covers such a wide range, elsewhere this expression has been used to designate certain other stages of realization.[25]

16. "One who develops the contemplation of danger abandons adherence (to formations) due to attachment" (*ādīnavānupassanaṁ bhāvento ālayābhinivesaṁ pajahati*).

One who develops meditation by repeatedly examining the dangers involved in formations relinquishes the adherence to formations with attachment. Both Vism. and PmA. identify this contemplation with knowledge of danger resulting from the knowledge of appearance as terror. PmA. further states that the contemplation of revulsion is also included within this contemplation of danger, which in turn is an aspect of the contemplation of suffering.

17. "One who develops the contemplation of reflection abandons non-reflection" (*paṭisaṅkhānupassanaṁ bhāvento appaṭisaṅkhaṁ pajahati*).

One who repeatedly sees with wisdom the three characteristics relinquishes delusion, here called "non-reflection."

Vism. Exp.: "The contemplation of reflection is the knowledge of reflection which effects the means to gain liberation from formations" (Vism. XXII,120).

PmA. Exp.: "The contemplation of reflection is a combination of the contemplations of impermanence, suffering, and non-self, resulting from the knowledge of desire for deliverance; it is undertaken for achieving liberation from formations. This contemplation comprises all the three insight knowledges of desire for deliverance, of reflection, and of equanimity towards formations."

18. "One who develops the contemplation of turning away abandons adherence due to bondage" (*vivaṭṭā nupassanaṁ bhāvento saṁyogābhinivesaṁ pajahati*).

The person who develops the contemplation on turning away from formations, inclining towards Nibbāna, relinquishes the strong adherence to formations that results from intimate association with them.

Vism.Exp.: "The contemplation of turning away comprises the two knowledges of equanimity about formations (*saṅkhār' upekkhā-ñāṇa*) and conformity (*anuloma-ñāṇa*). Here the mind turns away and recoils from all formations."[26]

PmA.Exp.: "The contemplation of turning away is the knowledge of change-of-lineage (*gotrabhū*) resulting from the knowledge of conformity." (The absence of an adverting consciousness for the contemplation of turning away in the *Paṭisambhidāmagga* is the reason for this conclusion.)[27]

The knowledge of change-of-lineage occurs only in a single consciousness. If this is identical with the contemplation of turning away the problem arises of accommodating the idea of "repeatedly" implied by the term *anupassanā*. (It is true that the supramundane path wisdom occurring only in a single consciousness too has been referred to in the commentaries as the contemplations of dispassion, of cessation, and of relinquishment;[28] but these are only alternatives to the corresponding mundane contemplations.) The contemplation of turning away can be regarded as a contemplation of relinquishment.

Although a certain developmental sequence can be discerned in the seven contemplations, such a progression seems untenable in regard to the eighteen principal insights as a set. To posit a serial progression would lead to absurd conclusions. The contemplation of danger would then have to follow that of revulsion. Likewise, the contemplations of dispassion, of cessation, and of relinquishment are mature contemplations extending up to the consummation of insight. By introducing the contemplations of destruction, of fall, and of change after them, a retrogression in insight would be indicated. In the Buddha's discourses the contemplations of destruction and of fall are generally cited before those of dispassion, cessation, and relinquishment.[29]

Even the contemplations of the signless, the desireless, and voidness turn out to be gateways to liberation which become functional at the acme of insight meditation. Hence the insight into phenomena that is higher wisdom, correct knowledge and vision, and contemplation of danger cannot follow them temporally, for this would indicate a relapse. Further, as was shown earlier, the insight into phenomena that is higher wisdom and correct knowledge and vision are not individual contemplations confined to a particular stage but general terms covering a wide range of insights. Similarly, even the contemplation of reflection, in the literal sense, can be taken as an umbrella term. At the same time several of the contemplations are very similar to one another (e.g. the contemplations of destruction and of fall).

Such being the case, it would be better to take this series of eighteen principal insights, not as a linear succession of contemplations, but as a compendium of contemplations drawn from various sources. Several of these sets partly overlap. The three contemplations of impermanence, of suffering, and of non-self have been placed at the head of the list, for they constitute the pivotal foundation common to the entire system of insight meditation. Because they pervade the path of insight in its entirety, these three may even be treated as an independent system of insight meditation.

Next, the series comprising the contemplations of impermanence, of suffering, of non-self, of revulsion, and of dispassion, comprises another prominent system of insight meditation. The contemplations of impermanence, of dispassion, of cessation, and of relinquishment make up still another significant group. There is another series obtained by appending the contemplation of fall (*vaya*) to the last-mentioned fourfold group (see S.iv,211–12). A few more such classifications within the seven principal contemplations were mentioned earlier in Chapter 8.

The sevenfold group comprises another major system. Several additional groups also have been created by combining some of the seven with the contemplations of destruction and of fall (e.g. impermanence, suffering, non-self, destruction, fall, dispassion, cessation, and relinquishment: A.v,360–61; destruction, decay, dispassion, cessation: S.ii,60). At times the contemplation of change is also added (e.g. impermanence, destruction, fall, dispassion, cessation, change: S.iv,216–17).

Yet another important categorization is made up of correct knowledge and vision, revulsion, and dispassion. Different systems of insight meditation can be improvised from the discourses wherein the term *saññā* (= perception) has been used to denote a method of meditation (e.g. the perceptions of impermanence, of non-self, of foulness, of danger, of abandonment, of dispassion, of cessation: D.ii,79; iii,253, 282).

Many systems of insight meditation of this type, occurring in the discourses of the Buddha, can be incorporated into the eighteen principal insights. Therefore we can infer that this series of eighteen insights is a compendium which the ancient teachers compiled by combining the meditations designated as contemplations with other meditations which, although not referred to as such, still belong to the same general category.

The succession of eighteen principal insights can also be analysed as a graded series with several phases of progress. A meditator endowed with good moral strength obtained through the practice of the perfections (*pāramī*) can easily fulfil the first three contemplations, followed by a sharp contemplation of revulsion; thereafter he can achieve the consummation of insight through the contemplation of dispassion. One who fails in this undertaking will have to develop all the seven contemplations. If he still fails, he will have to progress further in the contemplations of destruction, of fall, and of change and then achieve consummation of insight through one of the three contemplations—of the signless, of the desireless, or of voidness. The higher wisdom of insight into phenomena can be said to represent all the contemplations mentioned here. And then correct knowledge and vision, followed by the contemplations of danger, of reflection, and of turning away can be cited as comprising still another independent system.

The path of insight may also be brought to maturity by practising any contemplation suited to the occasion instead of following an accepted but rigid pattern. This is what is applicable to the ordinary meditator.

The *Paṭisambhidāmagga* often presents the path of insight through the eighteen principal insights, yet it does not furnish an exegetical analysis of them. This suggests that at the time the *Paṭisambhidāmagga* was compiled, this series of principal contemplations may have been used so widely that a precise analysis of them was thought unnecessary. But it is a cause for wonder that there is no reference to this group of eighteen insights elsewhere in the Sutta Piṭaka.

Even today the meditator can personally experience these principal insights, though all eighteen may not be commonly attested to by every meditator. A newcomer to insight meditation need not attempt the contemplations separately one by one. But at certain stages, if one suspects that one's progress has been retarded, it would be fruitful to pay special attention to a suitable contemplation.

Notes

Introduction

1. See Appendix 1: Conventional and Ultimate Truth.
2. See Appendix 2: Two Kinds of Knowledge.
3. Certain meditators, once they have made a little progress in their practice, think that they are now proficient enough to proceed on their own and no longer need to listen to the meditation master. As a result they lose their way and their meditation practice degenerates. To ensure success, one should always keep the teacher informed of one's progress and strictly follow his guidance. If any doubts arise about the teacher, his instructions, or the subject of meditation, the meditator should get them resolved immediately in a suitable manner; otherwise the meditation may stagnate.
4. Vism. (III,29ff.) enumerates ten impediments: (i) *abodes*—attachment to dwelling places; (ii) *family*—attachment to helpful relatives, friends, etc.; (iii) *gain*—receiving too many requisites; (iv) *group*—teaching a group or class of students; (v) *work*—tasks connected with putting up buildings; (vi) *travel*—travelling long distances; (vii) *kin*—family relations, teachers, pupils, colleagues, group-mates, etc., whom one is obliged to look after in time of illness; (viii) *affliction*—any kind of illness; (ix) *books*—being responsible for study, writing, etc.; (x) *supernormal powers*—the maintenance of which is an obstacle for insight meditation though not for tranquillity meditation. However, elsewhere (e.g. at KhuA.22) reputation (*kitti*) is mentioned as an alternative to supernatural powers.
5. See Appendix 3: The Four Protective Meditations.
6. The five hindrances (*pañca nīvaraṇā*) are: sensual lust, ill-will or anger, sloth and torpor, agitation and worry, and doubt. As these are the major obstacles to the development of concentration and wisdom, meditators have to guard against them very vigilantly. Many meditators fail to achieve progress owing to their inability to overcome these obsta-

cles. When confronted with the hindrances one must train oneself to identify them and eliminate them at once, determining to prevent them from re-emerging; for if a hindrance is allowed to surface repeatedly it will gather strength and become difficult to subdue.

7. For more on the jhānas, see Ven. Mahāthera Mātara Shri Ñāṇārāma, *The Seven Stages of Purification and the Insight Knowledges*, 2nd ed. (Kandy: BPS, 1993), pp.15–18. As stated in Vism. (III,105–7), the eight subjects of recollective meditation (*anussati*)—the Buddha, the Dhamma, and the Sangha; virtue (*sīla*), generosity (*cāga*), the gods (*devatā*), peace (*upasama*), and death (*maraṇa*)—as well as the perception of the repulsiveness of food (*āhāre paṭikkūla-saññā*), and attention to elements (*dhātu-manasikāra*)—though unable to induce absorption (*appanā*), can engender access concentration (*upacāra-samādhi*) sufficiently strong to suppress the hindrances. One should embark on insight meditation with this access concentration as the basis. Vism. remarks further (at VII,121–27) that although the first six recollections succeed only with noble disciples, a virtuous worldling may use them to suppress the hindrances and then, on that basis, begin the practice of insight meditation. The recollection of peace is dealt with in the same way (Vism. VIII,250).

   One achieves the first jhāna alone through the ten perceptions of foulness (*asubha*) and mindfulness directed to the body (*kāyagatāsati*); the first three jhānas through loving-kindness (*mettā*), compassion (*karuṇā*), and altruistic joy (*muditā*), and the fourth jhāna only through equanimity (*upekkhā*). All the four jhānas are attainable through the ten *kasiṇas* and mindfulness of breathing (*ānāpāna-sati*). The four immaterial states (*āruppa*), as subjects of meditation, are specific for the corresponding four immaterial jhānas (Vism. III,107).

8. A jhāna attainer may remain attached to the bliss and calm of the jhānas and fail to take up insight meditation. Here one should specially bear in mind that not only jhānic bliss but even birth in the Brahma-worlds through the power of jhāna is impermanent. The aim of Buddhism is not serenity but the peace of the path, fruition, and Nibbāna, which is attainable only through insight-wisdom. Hence one should

devote oneself to insight meditation. It may be easy to make progress in serenity meditation if one can initially subdue the defilements to a certain degree through insight meditation. However, some meditators who are solely accustomed to insight meditation might occasionally find it difficult or disagreeable to practise serenity meditation.

9. The defilements, including the hindrances, are generally eliminated in three main stages: (i) through the power of sense-sphere wholesome activity, one removes them by the "substitution of opposites" (*tadaṅga-pahāna*); (ii) through the power of the fine-material and immaterial sphere jhānas one removes them by suppression (*vikkhambhana-pahāna*); and (iii) through the power of the supramundane paths one completely eradicates them (*samuccheda-pahāna*). The supramundane paths cut off the defilements along with their underlying tendencies (*anusaya*) so that they can never arise again. The first two methods eliminate the defilements temporarily, only for as long as the corresponding wholesome activity is operative. Since the underlying tendencies have not been eradicated, the suppressed defilements may later re-emerge. Insight meditation eliminates defilements through the "substitution of opposites" (*tadaṅga*), which paves the way for the final and complete eradication by the supramundane paths.

10. According to Pm.i,166ff., concentration, whether achieved through serenity meditation or insight meditation, should possess the following ten characteristics:

    (i) the mind is not distracted (*vikkhitta*) by pursuing the past;
    (ii) nor agitated (*kampita*) by longing for the future;
    (iii) nor shrunk through lethargy (*kusīta*);
    (iv) nor agitated through restlessness (*uddhacca*);
    (v) nor servile through passion (*rāga*);
    (vi) nor stubborn through anger (*vyāpāda*);
    (vii) the two pairs of faculties—confidence/wisdom and energy/concentration—should be in equilibrium;
    (viii) the faculties of confidence, energy, mindfulness, concentration, and wisdom should be directed towards a single purpose;

(ix) energy should be sufficient for the last two purposes;

(x) concentration should be strengthened through repeated practice.

The insight knowledges dawn only when the mental concentration is characterized by these qualities.

11. "Formations" (*saṅkhārā*) denotes everything produced through causes and conditions, hence everything comprised by the two terms "mind" and "matter" (*nāma* and *rūpa*). The ultimate entities (*paramattha*) designated "mind" (*nāma*) are the eighty-nine states of consciousness (*citta*) and the fifty-two mental factors (*cetasika*); "matter" (*rūpa*), the twenty-eight ultimate material phenomena. This same psycho-physical complex is also analysed into the five aggregates, the four immaterial aggregates—feeling, perception, mental formations (= all mental factors except feeling and perception), and consciousness—constituting *nāma*; the aggregate of matter constitutes *rūpa*. This same psycho-physical complex is also sub-divided into twelve sense bases (*āyatana*), six or eighteen elements (*dhātu*), and so on.

The Buddha had to introduce these separate classifications to suit the varying intellectual capacities of the beings needing his instructions. It should be noted that "formations" (*saṅkhārā*) is used above in two different senses: (i) as all conditioned phenomena, and (ii) as the fourth of the five aggregates. To distinguish them we refer to (ii) as "mental formations." *Saṅkhārā* is used in the formula of dependent arising (*paṭicca-samuppāda*) to refer to "kamma-formations," kammically active volitions.

12. The sutta is found at A.ii,94. The three Pāli terms in the catechism are: *daṭṭhabba*, *sammasitabba*, and *vipassitabba*. Since at Pug. 61–62 the insight-attainer is defined as one who has attained a supramundane state, we can conclude that the catechism quoted here covers the whole path of insight.

13. "Full understanding" in the mundane sense is threefold: (i) full understanding of the known (*ñāta-pariññā*); (ii) full understanding as investigation (*tīraṇa-pariññā*); and (iii) full understanding as abandoning (*pahāna-pariññā*). For details see Vism. XX,3–4.

14. The "corruptions of insight" are ten extraordinary experiences that arise when insight meditation begins to gather momentum, particularly in the tender phase of the knowledge of rise and fall: the perception of an aura around oneself, sharp increase in understanding, zest, tranquillity, happiness, confidence, energy, mindfulness, equanimity, and strong attachment to these states. Some meditators may encounter only a few of them. It is the attachment which turns these into "corruptions," for when one becomes attached to them one may presume that one has achieved some supramundane realization and may even neglect one's own meditation in order to teach others. Here the danger lies not in the experiences themselves, but in the enjoyment of them and the misconceptions about their significance. To avoid these pitfalls one must contemplate such experiences in the light of the three characteristics and seek the teacher's help when necessary.

15. See note 13.

16. At this point the meditator may be able to harness for further progress the powerful insight that has been built up in his mental continuum through the realization of the path and fruit of stream-entry. Accordingly, he may temporarily drop his concern for mastering the fruit of the first path and resume insight meditation with the aim of attaining the second path, that of once-returning. This will generate the series of insight knowledges with even sharper penetration than on the earlier occasion, thereby providing the necessary basis for the arising of the second path. In this manner the meditator might attempt to extend the practice of insight meditation even up to arahantship.

    A meditator who cannot do this should, after realizing the first path, master the attainment of fruition. This will help to consolidate the insight knowledges in their proper sequence. (If the meditator does not attend to this punctually he might find it difficult to regain fruition on a later occasion.) Once the attainment of fruition has been firmly established, he should not pursue it further but should instead arouse insight for the attainment of the next path. (If any concern with the previous fruition were to linger on he might revert to it and become confused.) In this manner insight will continue on to its consummation with the gradual realization of arahantship. See *The Seven Stages of Purification* for a detailed discussion of the purifications and insight knowledges.

17. See note 13.
18. See note 9.
19. *Anupassatī ti anu anu passati, anekehi ākārehi punappunaṁ passatī ti attho* (Vism. XXI,14; PmA.182).
20. Pm.i,54, 57, 58; Vism. XXI,1.
21. Pm.i,20, 24, 25, 32, 47, etc. An English translation of Pm. by Bhikkhu Ñāṇamoli is published under the title *The Path of Disrimination* (PTS, 1982).
22. Pm.i,10, 211; ii,42–43, 241–42.
23. Vism. XX,90; XXII,113, DA.i,47–48; AṬ.ii,275, etc.
24. Pm.i,10, 56, 57-58, 76–78; ii,185–86.
25. E.g. Vism. VIII,233, XX,4; MA.i,141–42; SṬ.ii,453–54.

Chapter 1: Contemplation of Impermanence

1. "Bhikkhus, there are these three characteristics that mark the conditioned as conditioned. What three? An arising is discerned, a passing away is discerned, an alteration of what persists is discerned" (A.i,152). See also S.iii,37–40.
2. "When the aggregates are born, decay, and die, moment by moment, you, bhikkhu, are born, decay, and die" (KhuA.50).
3. Certain highly meritorious people who have trained their minds over a long time in saṁsāra and fulfilled the *pāramīs* (perfections) can realize Nibbāna merely by listening to an exposition of the Dhamma. Even while listening they can purify their virtue, gain concentration, and awaken insight sufficient to attain Nibbāna. This is substantiated by suttas such as the Bāhiya Sutta (Ud.8, UdA.63), the Vimuttāyatana Sutta (A.iii,21ff., AA.ii,588), and the Saṅgiti Sutta (D.iii,241ff., DA.ii,756). Not only by listening to the Dhamma but also by preaching, reciting, pondering over the teaching, or even by a lucid understanding of any subject of meditation one can generate rapture through comprehending the Dhamma. By further developing this state one can achieve access concentration, on the basis of which one can practise insight

meditation and attain arahantship, as explained in the Vimuttāyatana Sutta and its commentary (see above). Only those who exert themselves diligently with the supportive strength of the *pāramīs* can achieve Nibbāna so swiftly. For most people the realization of Nibbāna must occur through the earnest practice of meditation for an extended period until the requisites of enlightenment (*bodhipakkhiyā dhammā*) reach maturity.

4. The perception of impermanence (*anicca-saññā*) is explained in the Girimānanda Sutta (A.v,109): "And what, Ānanda, is the perception of impermanence? Here, Ānanda, a bhikkhu who has gone to a forest or to the foot of a tree or to an empty hut considers thus: 'Material form is impermanent. Feeling ... Perception ... Mental formations ... Consciousness is impermanent.' Thus he dwells contemplating impermanence in regard to the five aggregates of grasping. This is called the perception of impermanence." See too DA.ii,757; DṬ.74.

5. Pm.i,171. The commentary adds that the meditator with a long nose should select the tip of the nose; one with a short nose, the upper lip (PmA.328).

6. *Sabbakāyapaṭisaṁvedī assasissāmī'ti sikkhati; sabbakāyapaṭisaṁvedī passasissāmī'ti sikkhati*: (D.ii,291; M.i,56). "'Experiencing the whole (breath-) body, I shall breathe in,' thus he trains himself. 'Experiencing the whole (breath-) body I shall breathe out,' thus he trains himself." The term "whole (breath-) body" refers to the entire mass of in-breathing and out-breathing, not to the physical body. Vism. VIII,171 further explains that the meditator should be conscious of the beginning, the middle, and the end of each inhalation and exhalation. To accomplish this, he should keep his attention fixed exclusively on the point where the breath is felt, either the nose tip or the upper lip. Further details are given at Vism. VIII,198ff. At Pm.i,164 the meditator is warned not to follow the breath in its passage inside the body, as this can be an obstacle to concentration. Therefore the beginning of a breath is the moment it initially touches the tip of the nose or the upper lip; the end is the moment the touch sensation ceases; and the middle is the phase between these two points.

7. "The characteristic of impermanence does not become apparent because, when rise and fall are not given attention, it is concealed by continuity" (Vism. XXI,3).
8. "The perception of impermanence, etc., are accomplished by one who, by means of the discernment of mentality-materiality and the overcoming of doubt, has removed the obstructive delusion and thereby becomes established in the full understanding of the known" (DṬ.73).
9. "When continuity is disrupted by discerning rise and fall, the characteristic of impermanence becomes apparent in its true nature" (Vism. XXI,4).
10. "All formations are impermanent. Why? Because of the occurrence of rise and fall, because of change, because of temporariness, and because of preclusion of permanence" (Vism. XX,47). See also MA.ii,93.
11. To facilitate the discernment of conditions (*paccaya-pariggaha*), after discerning mentality-materiality the meditator should expand his attention by noting intention. Before any action one should note the intention to act, e.g. before raising one's hand one should first note the intention to raise the hand. Initially this requires a deliberate effort, but with practice the noting becomes spontaneous. This helps to clarify how mind and matter function in a cause-and-effect relationship, i.e. because of the intention the act of raising the hand occurs.
12. See the Channa Sutta (S.iii,132–33) and its commentary (SA.ii,232).
13. See A.ii,33–34; S.iii,85.
14. The texts enumerate eleven methods whereby the characteristic of impermanence can be comprehended by way of groups: "Whatever material form is (i–iii) past, present, or future, (iv–v) internal or external, (vi–vii) gross or subtle, (vii–ix) inferior or superior, (x–xi) distant or close—all such material form one defines as impermanent. This is the first form of comprehension..." (Pm.i,53). The other four aggregates are similarly comprehended. The range over which the comprehension by groups extends depends on the strength of the meditator's wisdom.

15. Knowledge of rise and fall is consummated in fifty ways. First the comprehension of the origination of materiality occurs by way of five observations: (i) by observing the characteristic of origination; (ii–v) by observing that materiality originates because of ignorance, craving, kamma, and nutriment. Next, the cessation of materiality is comprehended in five ways: (i) by observing the characteristic of change inherent in materiality; (ii–v) by observing that materiality ceases by the cessation of each of the same four conditions. The observation of the rise and fall of the mental aggregates also occurs in this same tenfold manner, but mentality-materiality (*nāma-rūpa*) replaces nutriment as a condition for the aggregate of consciousness, contact (*phassa*) as a condition for the three aggregates of feeling, perception, and mental formations (Pm.i,54–57).

16. With conformity knowledge (*anuloma-ñāṇa*) one of the three contemplations of impermanence, suffering, or non-self becomes prominent, immediately after which the meditator experiences Nibbāna. This experience is called liberation (*vimokkha*). The aspect of Nibbāna that is experienced depends on the contemplation that emerged with conformity knowledge. Hence, at the stage of conformity, the three contemplations are called doors of liberation (*vimokkha-mukha*). If the door is the contemplation of impermanence, the signless liberation (*animitta-vimokkha*) arises; if it is the contemplation of suffering, the desireless liberation (*appaṇihita-vimokkha*) arises; if it is the contemplation of non-self, the void liberation (*suññata-vimokkha*) arises (Pm.ii,48; Vism. XXI,66ff.).

17. Pm.i,30-31. On how these four factors occur in relation to the contemplations, see Pm.i,32-33. In every aspect of both *samatha* and *vipassanā* meditation the fulfilment of these four conditions brings success.

18. See Introduction, note 9.

19. A.ii,52; Pm.ii,80. All three distortions are extirpated with the attainment of stream-entry: Pm.ii,81; Vism. XXII,68.

20. A.iii,443.

Chapter 2: Contemplation of Suffering

1. M.i,232.
2. *Udayabbayaparipīḷitattā*. Vism. XVI,35. See too Vism. XXI,7.
3. On the various classifications of suffering, see Vism. XVI,35.
4. All objects conceived by the mind, apart from sense objects, are collectively designated "mental objects" or "objects of thought" (*dhammārammaṇa*). This embraces all formations, Nibbāna, and all concepts and ideas (*paññatti*).
5. "Pleasant feelings are designated 'suffering due to change' because they are a cause for the arising of pain owing to their changing nature" (Vism. XVI,35).
6. In several of the Buddha's discourses the contemplation of suffering has been referred to as "the perception of suffering in impermanence" (*anicce dukkha-saññā*): e.g. A.iii,334, 452; iv,52; D.iii,243, 251; S.v,132. See too DA.ii,757; AA.ii,665.
7. See Vism. XXI,3, 4, and VismṬ.ii,437.
8. At S.iv,259 the Venerable Sāriputta says: "Friend, there are these three forms of suffering, namely, intrinsic suffering (*dukkhadukkhatā*), suffering due to formations (*saṅkhāra-dukkhatā*), and suffering due to change (*vipariṇāma-dukkhatā*)." Vism. XVI,34 enumerates four more forms of suffering: concealed or exposed, and direct or indirect. Even these can be included within the aforementioned threefold suffering.
9. "But since arisen formations have arrived at presence and when present are afflicted by aging and on arriving at aging are bound to dissolve, they are therefore painful because of continual oppression, because of being hard to bear, because of being the basis of suffering, and because of precluding pleasure" (Vism. XX,47). See also MA.ii,93.
10. Some meditators temporarily change their postures or readjust their bodily alignment to ease their pain. This habit deprives them of the opportunity to realize the true nature of suffering. When one realizes that the feeling of pain is merely a formation (*saṅkhāra*) and not something to be grasped as "I" or "mine," the subjective grasp of "I" and "mine" that engulfs the painful feeling is loosened. One then experiences merely the nature of pain. By enduring severely

painful feelings one fortifies one's concentration. If one remains steadily in one posture for about two hours, unshaken and with attention fixed on one's meditation object, the feeling loses its oppressive nature and concentration becomes stronger. In this state insight contemplation can function quite effectively.

11. "For him gladness arises. For one who is gladdened rapture arises. For one elated by rapture the body becomes calm. One calm in body feels happiness. For one who is happy the mind is concentrated" (A.iii,21–24, etc.).

12. A.iv,14. See too AA.ii,700.

13. The four *iddhipāda*, "roads to power" or "bases for success," included in the thirty-seven requisites of enlightenment, are: the intention (*chanda*) to continue one's spiritual exercises; effort (*viriya*) to maintain the unbroken continuity of meditation; consciousness (*citta*) always bent on meditation; and investigation (*vīmaṁsā*) or sustained inquiry. These become roads to power when they are practised without break from the beginning to the end of the meditation. It is by fulfilling the *iddhipādas* that meditation is perfected. If at least one of the four is sufficiently strengthened, the others too will mature and produce the desired results.

14. A.ii,52; Pm.ii,80. Distortion of views (*diṭṭhi-vipallāsa*) disappears completely with the attainment of stream-entry (Pm.ii,81), while the distortions of perception (*saññā*) and of consciousness (*citta*) disappear with the attainment of arahantship (Vism. XXII,68).

15. A.iii,443. According to the commentary (AA.ii,695), those who are still in training engage in loving ministration (*mettāvatāya*) to the Master; those who have attained arahantship have *fulfilled* loving ministration to him.

Chapter 3: Contemplation of Non-self

1. *na* + *attā* = *an* + *attā* = *anattā*. Here *na* is a negative prefix and the word *attā* refers to the "apparent self," "person," "being," etc. Pāli texts also employ *attā* in the sense of "oneself," "mind," "body," the collective unit of the aggregates during a single lifetime. In such contexts the term is a mere

conventional expression without any egoistic connotations. The Buddha says, "These, Citta, are worldly designations, worldly terms, worldly expressions, worldly concepts, by means of which the Tathāgata expresses himself without clinging to them" (D.i,202). See too M.i,500.

2. Some important sources for the doctrine of non-self are the Anattalakkhaṇa Sutta (S.iii,66-68), the Alaggadupama Sutta (M.i,130–42), the Cūḷasaccaka Sutta (M.i,227–37), the Mahārāhulovāda Sutta (M.i,420–26), and the Chachakka Sutta (M.iii,280–87). If, on certain occasions, the Buddha kept silent when asked about the self, we should understand that he adopted silence for one of three reasons: (i) it was not an opportune time to reply; (ii) the question was wrongly framed; or (iii) the question was not oriented towards Nibbāna. For the most noteworthy example, see S.iv,400–1.

3. See M.i,230–33; A.ii,164–65; S.iv,2, 3, etc.

4. See M.i,258–64; S.iv,167, etc.

5. See M.i,232–33; M.iii,282–84; S.iii,21–24.

6. S.iv,202–3. See also SA.iii,82.

7. The terms "imagine" (*maññati*) and "imagining" (*maññita*) imply conceiving the five aggregates—or, more broadly, any aspect of experience—by way of craving, conceit, and views (*taṇhā-māna-diṭṭhi*). The term *papañcita*, "conceptual proliferation," just below, is virtually synonymous with *maññita* (see MA.i,23). *Papañcita* is the past participle of *papañceti* (from the root *paci*, in the sense of "spreading out") and here implies the idea of a perverted concept. On the term *papañca*, see Bhikkhu Ñāṇananda, *Concept and Reality in Early Buddhist Thought* (BPS, 1971).

8. M.i,109–10; A.iv,9; Vism. XXII,60. As to the manner of their gradual disappearance with the development of the path, see Vism. XXII,64.

9. See Sabbāsava Sutta, the section on *saṁvara-pahāna* (M.i,9–10) and its commentary (MA.i,70–72).

10. M.i,111–12.

11. M.i,1. See also the commentary, MA.i,23, translated in Bhikkhu Bodhi, *Discourse on the Root of Existence*, 2nd. ed. (BPS, 1992), pp.5–12.

12. The three defilements—craving (*taṇhā*), conceit (*māna*), and views (*diṭṭhi*)—occur in the unwholesome states of mind rooted in greed (*lobha*). Craving (the mental factor of greed) occurs in every state of mind rooted in greed. Sometimes it occurs without conceit and views, at other times with one or the other, but never with both simultaneously. Nevertheless, though occurring separately, conceit and views may reinforce each other. The proximate causes for the three imaginings are: feeling, for the imagining of craving; perception, for the imagining of views; and applied thought (*vitakka*), for the imagining of conceit (UdA.248).
13. S.iii,46. See also SA.ii,196–97.
14. S.iii,105. Also SA.ii,225; AA.ii,575.
15. The Khemaka Sutta (S.iii,126–32) explains that the non-returner (*anāgāmin*)—who has eliminated personality view (*sakkāya-diṭṭhi*) and sensual passion (*kāmarāga*)—still retains a subtle residue of the conceit "I am" (*asmimāna*), the desire "I am" (*asmichanda*), and the underlying tendency (*anusaya*) to egoistic thoughts. Thus, though the egoistic view "this am I" (*ayam aham asmi*) does not arise in him in relation to the five aggregates, he still harbours a subtle notion "I am" in relation to the five aggregates collectively (*samūhato pañcasu pi khandhesu asmī ti adhigato*: SA.ii,231). This notion "I am," generated by the extremely subtle operations of ignorance (*avijjā*), desire for becoming (*bhava-rāga*), and conceit (*māna*), may be regarded as the subtlest, most fundamental mode of the imagining "I am," which at a grosser level is responsible for the view of self (*atta-diṭṭhi*) in the unenlightened worldling.
16. S.iii,96.
17. SA.ii,196.
18. Pm.i,135; PmA.298–99. See also M.i,135; S.iii,204.
19. S.iii,46.
20. Personality view is treated in detail in Appendix 4. On personality view as a basis for the other types of speculative views, see S.iv,287.
21. The Buddha often shows how, because of the hollowness of personality view, the security and the stability built

thereon are easily shattered, to the consternation of the unenlightened worldling (e.g. M.i,8; 136–37; S.iii,15–18, 42, 138, etc.).

22. Certain thinkers extend the concept of the self to the past and the future through mere logical reasoning, while certain meditators settle on various views regarding the self as a result of misconstruing the signs (*nimitta*), absorptions (*jhāna*), higher knowledges (*abhiññā*), etc., produced by the development of tranquillity meditation. (See D.i,12–38 and its commentary DA.i,72–86, and also D.ii,64 and its commentary DA.i,345–46.) By accepting the teachings of such theorists uncritically, many other people become established in their views about the self.

23. S.iii,98.

24. The Brahmajāla Sutta enumerates the thirty-two eternalist views based on these five imaginings. With the addition of eighteen eternalist views relating to the past and five views on "Nibbāna in this very life," a total of fifty-five eternalist views are expounded in this discourse (D.i,12–38).

25. See Pm.i,159; It.43–44. The Brahmajāla Sutta elaborates seven annihilationist views (D.i,34–35). In the Alagaddupama Sutta (M.i,140–41) the Buddha rejects as false and baseless the charge that he is an annihilationist.

26. "Kaccāyana, the beings of this world usually base their views on two things: on existence and non-existence.... Imprisoned by the habit of pursuing, grasping, and settling in systems is this world.... 'Everything exists'—this is one extreme; 'nothing exists'—this is the other extreme. Avoiding both these extremes, the Tathāgata teaches the Dhamma by the middle" (S.ii,17; iii,134–35). SA.ii,25 explains the two extremes here as eternalism and annihilationism, respectively.

27. At Pm.i,138 the causes and conditions responsible for the generation of views (*diṭṭhi*) have been summarized as eightfold: (1) the five aggregates; (2) ignorance; (3) contact; (4) perception; (5) applied thought; (6) unwise attention; (7) bad company; and (8) listening to others' views. PmA.299–300 cites examples for these.

The way to abandon views of self lies in the cessation of the false imagination, as explained by the Buddha at S.iv,24:

"Monks, whatever is imagined (to be the self) or wherever (the self) is imagined to exist or whatever (the self) is imagined to be external to, or whatever is imagined to be 'mine'—all these become otherwise. However, beings attached to becoming, which has the nature to change, find delight in this same becoming. Monks, so far as there are aggregates, elements, or sense spheres, one does not imagine them (to be self), nor does one imagine (the self) as inside them or outside them or as 'mine.' By not imagining thus, one does not grasp anything in the world. Not grasping, one does not become agitated through craving. Not being agitated, one fully realizes Nibbāna in this very life (through the complete extinction of defilements). Then one comes to know: 'Destroyed is birth; lived is the holy life; done is what should be done; nothing further remains to be done.' Monks, this is the proper practice that enables one to eradicate all imaginings."

28. Vism. XX,47. See too VismṬ.ii,407; MA.ii,94.

29. The term element (*dhātu*) denotes a subtle phenomenon devoid of any nature of a being or a self. As cohesion (water) is subtler than the other three primary elements, initially it may be harder to understand. Therefore, when contemplating the elements, one must consider that the water element has the nature of binding the earth element. As mindfulness, concentration, and wisdom develop, conviction through direct experience will dawn. The meditator will comprehend the various kinds of material form derived from these four primary elements according to the level of his intelligence.

30. As an example, let us suppose you have fixed your attention on the movement of the abdomen. The elements of earth, fire, air, or water that you discern in the present moment belong to the aggregate of material form; the cognizing mind belongs to the aggregate of consciousness. The faculty identifying the object, occurring in the same mind-moment, belongs to the aggregate of perception. The coexistent mental factor which experiences the object as pleasurable, painful, or neutral—to the aggregate of feeling. All the other coexistent mental phenomena headed by volition—to the aggregate of mental formations (M.i,190). When the mind

takes an immaterial object the supportive heart-base (*hadaya-vatthu*) pertains to the aggregate of matter. In this way it becomes clear in insight meditation how the five aggregates are always present collectively—a fact which certain meditators realize only at an advanced stage. Thereby it becomes possible to contemplate the five aggregates collectively as a single whole.

31. "Ānanda, what is the perception of non-self? Herein, Ānanda, a monk resorts to a forest or to the foot of a tree or to an empty house and reflects thus: 'Eye and forms, ear and sounds, nose and smells, tongue and tastes, body and touches, mind and mental objects—all these are non-self.' In this manner he lives contemplating the nature of non-self in the six internal and external sense spheres. Such, Ānanda, is the perception of non-self" (A.v,109).

In some texts the contemplation of non-self is referred to as "the perception of non-self in suffering"—*dukkhe anatta-saññā* (D.iii,243, 251; S.v,133; A.iii,85 etc.). Also it is said in the commentaries: "The perception of non-self in suffering is the perception arisen in the contemplative knowledge of non-self" (*dukkhe anatta-saññā' ti anattānupassanā-ñāṇe uppanna-saññā*; DA.ii,757; AA.ii,665).

32. Pm.ii,80-81; Vism. XXII,68.

33. "Having abandoned entirely the underlying tendency to passion and dispelled the underlying tendency to aversion, having uprooted the underlying tendency to the view and conceit 'I am,' having abandoned ignorance and aroused knowledge, he puts an end to suffering in this very life" (M.i,47).

The commentary (MA.i,186) explains: "The expression 'underlying tendency to the view and conceit "I am"' means the underlying tendency to conceit *which is similar to a view* (*diṭṭhisadisaṁ mānānusayaṁ*). This is said because the tendency to conceit is similar to a view in that it occurs based on the notion 'I am.' "

See too the Khemaka Sutta (S.iii,126–32) and note 15 above, and also the second division of the Mūlapariyāya Sutta (M.i,3–4).

34. A.iii,444. See also AA.ii,695.

Chapter 4: Contemplation of Revulsion

1. The revulsion that arises through insight must be distinguished from unwholesome revulsion, which is an aspect of aversion (*paṭigha*) or hatred (*dosa*).
2. M.i,509ff.
3. S.iii,21. Parallel passages follow dealing with suffering and non-self.
4. S.iii,22–23.
5. S.iii,19–20. The same is said regarding suffering and non-self.
6. S.iii,23. In the same manner he develops revulsion towards the aggregates after seeing their characteristics of suffering and non-self.
7. S.ii,95.
8. S.ii,96-97.
9. S.iv,32-33.
10. M.iii,278ff; S.iv,106–7.
11. S.iv,19–20.
12. S.iii,189.
13. S.ii,248–49.
14. S.iv,140.
15. The following texts make clear the dangers (*ādīnava*) in formations: "As all material form is impermanent, suffering, and subject to change—this is the danger in material form...." (S.iii,28). "Monks, because there is danger in material form, people develop revulsion towards material form" (S.iii,30).

    The same formula is applied to the other aggregates as well. The texts referred to in notes 4, 10, and 13 above show how the formations are devoid of a self owing to their being subject to impermanence, suffering, and change. The three characteristics—of impermanence, suffering, and non-self—constitute the dangers inherent in formations, by highlighting which one can generate revulsion.
16. A.v,311ff.; S.ii,30; A.v,315ff.
17. At SA.ii,40 it is said that correct knowledge and vision

(*yathābhūta-ñāṇadassana*) extends from the knowledge of the definition of mentality-materiality (*nāmarūpapariccheda-ñāṇa*) to the knowledge and vision of what is path and non-path (*maggāmagga-ñāṇadassana*). This embraces three stages: the penetration of individual characteristics (*paccattalakkhaṇa-paṭivedha*), the discernment of conditions (*paccaya-pariggaha*), and the penetration of the universal characteristics (*sāmañña-lakkhaṇa-paṭivedha*). See also Appendix 5, §15.

18. AA.ii,587, 676, 725; SA.ii,40, etc. SA takes revulsion here as meaning strong insight (*balava-vipassanā*), that is, the four insight knowledges: the appearance of terror (*bhayat'upa-ṭṭhāna*), contemplation of danger (*ādīnavānupassanā*), desire for deliverance (*muñcitukamyatā*), and equanimity about formations (*saṅkhār'upekkhā*). At Pm.ii,63 it is said that the knowledges of appearance of terror and of danger, as well as revulsion, are one and the same in meaning; they differ only in name. Vism. XXI,1, 29–43 describes these as three successive insight knowledges. MA.ii,94 identifies revulsion (*nibbidā*) with the insight leading to the emergence of the transcendental path (*vuṭṭhānagāminī vipassanā*). Certain commentarial contexts indicate that *nibbidā* is a common term referring to insight (DA.ii,477; PmA.152, 316, etc.).

19. Pm.i,57–58.

20. Pm.i,195 states: "One contemplating impermanence knows and sees in-breath as it is, thus there is knowledge of revulsion.... The wisdom of appearance of terror due to in-breath in one contemplating impermanence is knowledge of what is in conformity with revulsion.... The wisdom of reflexion and composure due to in-breath in one contemplating impermanence is knowledge as tranquillization of revulsion" (trans. after Ven. Ñāṇamoli). PmA.363–64 demonstrates how this series of knowledges connected to revulsion extends from comprehension in groups (*kalāpasammasana-ñāṇa*) to the consummation of insight.

21. "Through revulsion one becomes dispassionate, whereby one achieves liberation. When liberated one realizes that one is liberated" (M.i,500). MA.ii,95, commenting on this passage, identifies the onset of dispassion with the supramundane path.

22. Thag. 267–69.
23. *Nandin' ti sappītikaṁ taṇhaṁ* (Vism. XXI,19).
24. M.i,266–67. Similar discourses are found at M.iii,267ff.; S.iii,14, etc. See too MA.ii,259.
25. On the expression "perception of distaste for the whole world" (*sabbaloke anabhirata-saññā*) see A.i,41, 42; ii,150; iii,79; iv,46, 50; v,111; M.i,336. AA.ii,540 explains "world" (*loka*) here as the triple world (*tedhātuka*)—the sensuous, fine-material, and immaterial realms of the Buddhist cosmos; "distaste" (*anabhirati*), as lack of desire for life in these three realms. AṬ.ii,342 confirms that this perception is the contemplation of revulsion. See too Chap. 5, n.15.
26. A.i,51.

Chapter 5: Contemplation of Dispassion

1. For example, at Pm.ii,220 we find the following: "What are the five kinds of dispassion? Dispassion by suppression, dispassion by substitution of opposites, dispassion by extirpation, dispassion by subsiding, dispassion by emancipation. Dispassion by suppression occurs in regard to the five hindrances for one who develops the first jhāna; dispassion by substitution of opposites occurs in regard to views for one who develops concentration partaking of penetration (i.e. insight); dispassion by extirpation occurs for one who develops the supramundane path leading to destruction; dispassion by subsiding occurs at the moment of the fruit; dispassion by emancipation is the deathless element." See too PmA.513–15; AA.i,287. For further discussions see Pm.ii, 140ff., Vism. VIII,235; DA.ii,506; DṬ.330; PmA.177; ItA.190.
2. This kind of dispassion seems to be referred to in the following text: "Monks, without directly knowing and fully understanding all, without developing dispassion for all and abandoning all, one is incapable of eradicating suffering; but by directly knowing and fully understanding all, by developing dispassion for all and abandoning all, one is capable of eradicating suffering" (It.3–4). The commentary (ItA.42–43) demonstrates how this discourse encapsulates the entire path of insight meditation.

3. "Herein, 'fading away as destruction' is the momentary dissolution of formations. 'Absolute [ultimate] fading away' is Nibbāna" (Vism. VIII,235).

4. "Whatever phenomena there are, conditioned or unconditioned, dispassion is said to be the highest among them; that is, the end of craving, termination of passion, cessation (of formations), Nibbāna" (A.ii,34; It.88, etc.).

5. "Dispassion is the (supramundane) path.... Nibbāna is also dispassion. As all the phenomena arisen with Nibbāna as their object are also free from passion, these too are designated dispassion" (Pm.ii,140ff.).

6. At Pm.i,57-58 the seven contemplations are explained in relation to *bhaṅga-ñāṇa*, the knowledge of dissolution (see pp.98–99 in the present work). According to this explanation the contemplation of dispassion refers to dispassion through the substitution of opposites. Here there is no reference either to the momentary dissolution of phenomena (*khaya-virāga*) or to the supramundane dispassion. If the reference here were to *khaya-virāga* this would have been the best context to say so, for the latter appears in the knowledge of dissolution. Among the texts which confirm that *virāgānupassanā* here refers to *tadaṅga-virāga* are the following: PmA.64–65, 182; Vism. XXI,16; Vism.Ṭ.ii,441–42; DṬ.74; AA.ii,829; ItA.42–43; AṬ.ii,275. Outside the context of the seven contemplations, however, the commentaries sometimes explain the contemplation of dispassion in relation to *khaya-virāga*; see e.g. Vism. VIII,235; MA.ii,249; AA.ii,722.

7. (i) "Here, Ānanda, a bhikkhu ... reflects thus: 'This is the peaceful, this is the sublime, that is, the stilling of all formations, the relinquishment of all substrata of existence, the destruction of craving, dispassion, Nibbāna.' This is called the perception of dispassion" (A.v,110). *Virāga-saññā* in this context is described either as a subject of meditation on Nibbāna as peace (*upasama*: Vism. VIII,245ff.) or as a subject of meditation for entering into the attainment of fruition (*phala-samāpatti*: A.v,321–22, 354ff.). The perception of dispassion (*virāga-saññā*) is described as the perception generated in the contemplation of dispassion (DA.ii,757; AA.ii,665) and also as the perception generated in relation to the fivefold dispassion beginning with the suppression

(*vikkhambhana*) of defilements (AA.i,287ff.). See n.1 to the present chapter .

(ii) "The knowledge regarding the (Nibbānic) state of peace recognizes that there is suffering when there is occurrence (of formations) and happiness when there is no such occurrence (i.e. in Nibbāna)" (Pm.i,59; see too PmA.185).

8. MA.ii,249; AA.ii,722.

9. Pm.i,192; see too PmA.361.

10. Vism. VIII,235. Here the contemplation of dispassion is understood to imply two forms of dispassion: that of momentary dissolution and that of Nibbāna as the state completely free from passion. Thus "contemplation of dispassion" occurs as the seeing of both these aspects by way of insight and the supramundane path respectively.

11. (i) This is expressed in a verse:

> "Having known, 'This is suffering,'
> Of what is transient and disintegrating,
> Seeing its dissolution with wisdom,
> One becomes dispassionate towards it."
>
> (S.iv,205; see too SA.iii,83)

(ii) After defining the mundane dispassion as momentary dissolution, when describing the contemplation of dispassion in relation to mindfulness of breathing, PmA.347–48 says: "Here, 'contemplating dispassion' means (contemplating) with the insight that enables one to become dispassionate towards formations." See too n.13 below, and Chap. 8, n.17.

12. Henceforth when the term "dispassion" and the phrase "contemplation of dispassion" are used without qualification it is always dispassion through the substitution of opposites that is intended.

13. "The contemplation of dispassion by way of the contemplation of revulsion" (*virāgānupassanā'ti nibbidānupassanāvasena*)" (PmA.215).

14. A.iii,19, 200; iv.99, 336; v,2–6. The commentary says that in these instances *virāga* implies the supramundane path (AA.ii,587, 676, 725, 817). The point is discussed more fully later in this chapter (pp.67).

15. (i) A.v,111 succinctly explains *sabbaloke anabhirata-saññā* as follows: "Here, Ānanda, by abandoning any concern (*upaya*: craving, conceit, and view), clinging (*upādāna*: sensual lust, views, attachment to rituals, and belief in a self), established belief (*cetaso adhiṭṭhāna*: the two views of eternity and of annihilation), adherence (*abhinivesa*: self-view), and inherent unwholesome tendencies (the seven *anusaya*), one becomes disenchanted with the whole world."

    (ii) "Monks, when a monk lives often cultivating in mind the perception of distaste for the whole world, his mind bends away from the beautiful things in the world, recoils from them, draws back from them, refuses to go forward; either equanimity or revulsion becomes established" (A.iv,50).

    The relationship of this to the contemplation of revulsion was discussed in Chap.4, n.25 above.

16. "*Rāga*, etc., are synonyms for *lobha*; it is *rāga* in the sense of attachment, *nandi* in the sense of delighting, and *taṇhā* in the sense of craving" (SA.ii,85). See too MA.iv,65.

17. PmA.94.

18. S.iii,52. See too S.iv,142–44; SA.ii,197–98; iii,33.

19. S.ii,30. See too A.v,312–17.

20. SA.ii,40.

21. DA.ii,477; MA.ii,95; AA.ii,587, 676, 725, 817, etc. This commentarial tradition could have developed on the basis of the statement at Pm.ii,140ff. that *virāga* is the supramundane path and *vimutti* its fruition. Nevertheless, in the same text (Pm.ii,143) *vipassanā* too is called *virāga* in the sense of contemplating.

22. A.v,59. See too AA.ii,831–32.

23. This is explained in detail in (vi) at pp.52–53 above. It is shown there how at this stage revulsion and dispassion are developed towards mental phenomena.

24. M.iii,243. The equanimity referred to here, though explained as the equanimity of jhāna in the commentary (MA.iv, 188–89), can also be taken as the equanimity of insight conjoined with jhānic concentration. The liberative power of this discourse is demonstrated by the fact that Pukkasāti became a non-returner (*anāgāmin*) while listening to it.

25. See above p.67. SṬ.ii,222 explains that in the phrase "by the elimination of delight, passion is eliminated," the elimination of delight is the consummation of the function of insight, issuing in "insight leading to emergence" (*vuṭṭhāna-gāmini-vipassanā*); in the phrase "by the elimination of passion, delight is eliminated," the elimination of passion is the destruction of passion by the insight leading to emergence, and "the elimination of delight" the eradication of delight by the supramundane path. See too A.v,50-51 and AA.ii,829.
26. See Pm.i,195.
27. Pm.ii,47–48.
28. A.i,216.
29. S.v,133.

Chapter 6: Contemplation of Cessation

1. *Nirujjhati, nirujjhanaṁ, vā nirodho. Ni + rodha = nirodha.* "'It ceases' means it does not exist (*nirujjhatī ti na bhavati*)" (PmA.362).
2. S.iii,24-25.
3. "Cessation is twofold as momentary (temporary) cessation and final (permanent) cessation" (AA.ii,722).
4. The final cessation of all formations occurs with the extinction of the five aggregates upon the demise of the arahant. Nevertheless, at the stage of the supramundane path the cluster of defilements eliminated by each path also becomes extinct. Accordingly, these defilements (which are formations too), as well as the other formations that might have resulted from them, are also extinguished. In this sense the supramundane path is regarded as cessation by extirpation (*samuccheda-nirodha*) or cessation without further emergence (*anuppāda-nirodha*).
5. Five kinds of cessation are enumerated at Pm.ii,221. These are in effect the same as the five kinds of dispassion, on which see Chap.5, n.1 above.
6. "Contemplation of cessation is the contemplation of the cessation of formations" (DṬ.74). See too n.7 (i) just below.

7. (i) "Contemplation of cessation (*nirodhānupassanā*) means contemplation of dissolution (*bhaṅga*)" (PmA.215).

   (ii) "How does the wisdom that sees the recurrent dissolution of phenomena through reflection on the sense object turn out to be insight-wisdom? The mind that takes material form as object originates and ceases. Having reflected on the dissolution of that object, one contemplates the dissolution of that reflecting mind itself by means of the succeeding mind" (Pm.i,57). See also PmA.182; Vism. XXI,13.

8. Pm.i,58. See also PmA.183; Vism. XXI,21.

9. (i) "Here, Ānanda, a bhikkhu ... reflects thus: 'This is the peaceful, this is the sublime, that is, the stilling of all formations, the relinquishment of all substrata of existence, the destruction of craving, cessation, Nibbāna.' This is called the perception of cessation" (A.v,110-11).

   "*The perception of cessation* is the perception arisen in the knowledge contemplating cessation" (AA.ii,665).

   (ii) "The knowledge of the state of peace: 'Arising is fearful, non-arising is safety.... Accumulation of kamma is worldly, non-accumulation is unworldly.... The sign is formations, the signless is Nibbāna'" (Pm.i,59–60).

10. (i) "Having seen the danger in material form, he becomes desirous of the cessation of material form, he is resolute through faith, and his mind is well settled thereon; he trains thus, 'I shall breathe in contemplating cessation in material form'; he trains thus, 'I shall breathe out contemplating cessation in material form'" (Pm.ii,192).

    (ii) "*He develops the perception of cessation*: he develops the perception that arises making the cessation of formations the object. They also interpret this as the perception that arises making Nibbāna the object" (AA.i,287).

11. "Hence he says, 'By the contemplation of cessation one makes cease, one does not originate'; for this is desire for deliverance that has become strong" (DṬ.74).

12. "Then there remains only consciousness, purified and cleansed" (M.iii,242).

13. "Or contemplation of cessation is the contemplation, 'Those formations just cease; they do not arise by way of future origination'" (DṬ.74).

14. "Meghiya, when one is endowed with the perception of impermanence, the perception of non-self becomes established" (Ud.37; A.iv,358). See also A.iv,353 and M.i,424–25.

15. "After reflecting on the sense object one contemplates dissolution (*bhaṅga*) thereby realizing the voidness of formations: this is the insight that is higher wisdom" (Pm.i,58). For further explanations see Vism. XXI,23, 24; PmA.183.

16. "'He contemplates cessation': it should be understood that this is stated by way of insight through its ability to bring defilements to cessation" (PmA.347–48).

17. "Ignorance ceases with the cessation of its source ... with the cessation of its origin ... with the cessation of its genesis ... with the cessation of its production ... with the cessation of its cause ... with the cessation of its condition ... with the arousing of knowledge ... with the appearance of cessation" (Pm.ii,193).

18. *Virajaṁ vītamalaṁ dhammacakkhuṁ udapādi*: *Yaṁ kiñci samudayadhammaṁ sabbaṁ taṁ nirodhadhamman ti*. M.i,501; S.v,423, etc.

19. "Whatever there is that has come to be, conditioned, dependently arisen—the escape from it is cessation" (It.61; Pm.ii,221).

20. To ascertain whether a person has genuinely realized Nibbāna, several things have to be considered: (i) Whether, immediately after such experience, any form of reviewing knowledge (*paccavekkhana-ñāṇa*) occurs involuntarily. (ii) Whether, beginning with either the knowledge of the definition of mentality-materiality or the knowledge of rise and fall, one can enter and abide for a predetermined time in the successive insight knowledges and fruition attainment. (iii) Whether, at the realization of each insight knowledge, the ten characteristics enumerated in Chap. 1, n.10 are present. As experiences partly similar to the realization of Nibbāna may occur for various reasons, one has to be quite wary in coming to a judgement regarding this stage.

21. So it is said at PmA.94: "*Samudaya* is the origination of formations, by seeing their very dissolution in the contemplation of dissolution." See also Vism. XXI,16-17 and Vism.Ṭ. ii,442.

22. PmA.65. This seems to be based on Pm.i,57-58 and Vism. XXI,16–17.
23. "*Samudaya* refers to the origination of passion..." (PmA.94 = PmA.183).
24. "He contemplates dissolution. How does he contemplate? He contemplates as impermanent, not as permanent; he contemplates as suffering, not as happiness; he contemplates as non-self, not as self" (Pm.i,57-58).
25. At Pm.ii,46 it is said that the contemplations of impermanence and of non-self eliminate three forms of clinging (*upādāna*), and the contemplation of suffering only one, while the contemplation of cessation eliminates all four forms of clinging. This may be taken as an indication that the contemplation of cessation is an amalgamation either of all the three basic contemplations or of the contemplation of suffering with one of the other two.
26. MA.ii,249; AA.ii,722; Vism. VIII,235; Vism.Ṭ.i,28—81.
27. PmA.347–48.
28. PmA.177.
29. PmA.362. See also Pm.i,192ff.
30. Pm.ii,65–66.
31. S.v,133.

Chapter 7: Contemplation of Relinquishment

1. *Paṭi + ni + saj.*
2. Pm.i,194.
3. Pm.i,87. See too PmA.24, 211; VismṬ.i,281.
4. "The abandonment of material form is relinquishment as giving up (*pariccāga-paṭinissagga*). Similarly, the abandonment of feeling ... perception ... mental formations ... consciousness ... eye ... ear ... decay and death is relinquishment as giving up" (Pm.i,194). For the complete list, see Pm.i,5ff.
5. S.iv,29; Pm.i,27.
6. (i) "Seeing material form, he abandons. Seeing feeling ... perception ... mental formations ... consciousness ... the eye ... decay and death, he abandons" (Pm.i,27).

(ii) "O monks, whatever desire, lust, delight, or craving there is in you in regard to material form, abandon it; thus that form will be abandoned.... Whatever desire ... or craving there is in you in regard to consciousness, abandon it; thus that consciousness will be abandoned" (S.iii,161).

7. Vism. VIII,236; PmA.347.
8. *Nibbāne cittaṁ pakkhandatī ti pakkhandana-paṭinissaggo* (Pm.i,194).
9. Vism. VIII,236; PmA.347.
10. See VismṬ.i,279; DṬ.74.
11. See M.iii,187:

   "Let not a person revive the past
   Or on the future build his hopes;
   For the past has been left behind
   And the future has not been reached.
   Instead with insight let him see
   Each presently arisen state...."

12. "There is neither here nor there nor in between the two" (Ud.8).
13. "What is impermanent is suffering; what is suffering is impermanent. What is impermanent and suffering is non-self. What is impermanent, suffering, and non-self—that is 'such' (*tatha*). What is impermanent, suffering, non-self, and 'such'—that is truth (*sacca*). What is impermanent, suffering, non-self, 'such,' and truth—that is comprised in one (*ekasaṅgahita*). What is comprised in one—that is oneness (*ekatta*)" (Pm.ii,106).
14. "Monks, these four are realities (*tathāni*), not unrealities (*avitathāni*); they never become otherwise (*anaññathāni*). What four? Suffering, the origin of suffering, the cessation of suffering, and the path leading to the cessation of suffering" (S.v,430-31; Pm.ii,104). See too the commentarial gloss at SA.iii,228. The terms *tathatā, avitathatā, anaññathā* have also been cited as qualifying *paṭicca samuppāda*, dependent origination, at S.ii,26.
15. See M.i,135: "Even good qualities (*dhammā*) you should abandon, how much more then bad qualities (*adhammā*)?"

MA.ii,90 identifies the "good qualities" here with serenity and insight (*samatha-vipassanā*).

16. See Dhp.348:

> "Let go what is behind, let go what is in front,
> Let go in the middle, go beyond becoming.
> With a mind that is everywhere released
> Do not come again to birth and decay."

17. See Sn.1094, Dhp.89, A.v,110–11 (cited above, Chap. 6, n.9(i)).

18. Vism. VIII,236; PmA.347, etc.

19. For example: "Ānanda, what is the perception of abandonment? Here a monk … does not tolerate any evil unwholesome states that may arise; he abandons them, drives them away, relinquishes them, and terminates them—this is called the perception of abandonment" (A.v,110).

    Perception of abandonment (*pahāna-saññā*) refers to the fivefold abandonment (AA.i,287), i.e. by way of suppression, substitution of opposites, extirpation, subsiding, and emancipation (Pm.i,26: *vikkhambhana, tadaṅga, samuccheda, paṭippassaddhi, nissaraṇa*). These five terms are explained in the same way as the five kinds of dispassion and cessation—see Chap.5, n.1 and Chap.6, n.5. In insight meditation it is abandonment by substitution of opposites that is relevant. In this context perception of abandonment may be regarded as synonymous with contemplation of relinquishment. See DA.ii,757; AA.ii,665.

20. "He sees the abandonment of covetousness and grief (defilements rooted in craving and hatred) through his wisdom and becomes quite equanimous therein" (M.iii,84–85; S.v,324, 330–31, 337). For further explanation see MA.iv,98 or SA.iii,212.

21. "One who abandons defilements abandons the kamma based on them, and thereby the aggregates which would be produced through that kamma" (VismṬ.ii,442).

22. (i) "Contemplation of relinquishment is the stabilization of reflection" (DṬ.47).

    (ii) " 'He contemplates relinquishment': it should be understood that this is said by way of extremely sharp insight in the vicinity of the path" (PmA.348).

(iii) " 'He contemplates relinquishment': by way of insight leading to emergence" (PmA.215).

23. See PmA.94; DṬ.74; CNd.296.

24. "A self and what belongs to self are not to be found as real and valid" (M.i,138).

25. At Pm.ii,46-47 it is stated that contemplation of relinquishment is liberated from all four kinds of clinging; thus it seems to be an amalgamation of all three basic contemplations. PmA.393 explains that by abandoning defilements the contemplation of relinquishment frees one from all kinds of clinging.

26. M.i,477–501.

27. "One who has relinquished all is called 'one at peace'" (Sn.946).

28. M.i,140–41; S.iii,33. See too S.iv,80–82, where the same formula is applied to the six sense organs.

Chapter 8: Synopsis

1. Pm.i,57–58, 178, etc.
2. Pm.i,58. See also Vism. XXI,26; PmA.183–84.
3. Pm.ii,24f.: "Because of relinquishment there follows cessation" (*vossajjitattā tato nirujjhati*). See the commentarial gloss at PmA.380.
4. Pm.i,57.
5. Vism. XX,4.
6. Vism. XX,89ff. At SA.ii,83 it is said that all the seven contemplations become functional at the stage of the knowledge of comprehension (*sammasana-ñāṇa*).
7. Pm.i,20, 24–25, 32-33, 45–46, 169.
8. Pm.ii,232.
9. Pm.i,178, 183ff. The four final stages of this subject of meditation are the contemplations of impermanence, dispassion, cessation, and relinquishment. It is worth investigating why each of these has here been redefined in terms of the seven contemplations.
10. Pm.i,98ff; ii,172ff.

11. Pm.i,98-99. The attainment of cessation is the ability to suspend all consciousness for a pre-determined duration (up to a maximum of seven days). It can be achieved by a non-returner or an arahant who has mastered all the eight absorptions.

12. Pm.i,76ff.

13. *Aniccānupassī, dukkhānupassī,* and *anattānupassī*: S.iii,41; A.iv,13–14; A.v,109. *Nibbidānupassī*: A.i,50. *Aniccānupassī, virāgānupassī, nirodhānupassī, paṭinissaggānupassī*: M.i,251; iii,84; S.iv,212–14; v,324–37; A.iv,88, etc. *Aniccānupassī, dukkhānupassī, anattānupassī, khayānupassī, vayānupassī, virāgānupassī, nirodhānupassī, paṭinissaggānupassī*: A.v,359–61.

14. Relevant references are given in Chap.1, n.4; Chap.2, n.6, 12; Chap.3, n.31; Chap.4, n.25; Chap.5, n.7, 15, 29; Chap.6, n.9, 31; Chap.7, n.15. See too the passages cited at pp.25, 34–35, and 49.

15. D.iii,291; A.v,105; A.i,41.

16. D.ii,79; D.iii,251, 253, 283, 289-90; S.v,132-33; A.iii,79, 83–85, 334, 452; v.105, 106, etc.

17. *Idh'Ānanda bhikkhu sabbasaṅkhārehi aṭṭīyati harāyati jigucchati. Ayaṁ vuccat'Ānanda sabbasaṅkhāresu aniccasaññā* (A.v,11).

"Ānanda, herein a monk is troubled by, ashamed of, and disgusted with all formations: this is called the perception of impermanence in all formations." The text seems to imply the emergence of substitutional dispassion (*tadaṅga-virāga*), i.e. the removal of defilements through the substitution of opposites, by means of destructional dispassion (*khaya-virāga*), i.e. by contemplation of the momentary dissolution of formations.

18. (i) "He is practising for revulsion, dispassion, and cessation" (*nibbidāya, virāgāya, nirodhāya paṭipanno hoti*). S.ii,48; iii,19–20; A.i,64.

(ii) "It conduces to full revulsion, dispassion, cessation, tranquillity, higher knowledge, enlightenment, Nibbāna" (D.ii,251; A.i,30; iii,83, etc.).

19. *Aniccaṁ saṅkhataṁ paṭicca-samuppanaṁ, khayadhammaṁ vayadhammaṁ virāgadhammaṁ nirodhadhammaṁ*: M.i,500; S.ii,26; iii,24–25, etc.

20. M.i,6, iii,32ff; A.iii,452.
21. Pm.ii,283ff.
22. M.i,436; S.iii,167-69, 189; A.ii,128, etc. Some examples are quoted in Chaps. 3, 4, and 7.
23. Vism. XX,18ff., XXI 48, 59.
24. See Appendix 5.
25. Pm.ii,185. See the commentarial gloss at PmA.466.
26. Quoted from M.iii,302.

Appendixes

1. S.iii,159.
2. S.iii,101.
3. See e.g. M.i,300; S.iii,102.
4. Pm.i,143–49.
5. At M.i,66 the Buddha indicates that the outside spiritual teachers might gain some understanding of the clinging to sensual pleasures, to rules and observances, and to false views, but apart from a Fully Enlightened One and his disciples none can fully understand the clinging to a doctrine of self.
6. M.i,433.
7. S.iii,164–65.
8. S.iii,150, 151.
9. Pm.i,150–51.
10. Pm.i,195.
11. See e.g. MA.i,21.
12. Vism. XX,89-92; XXII,113–21.
13. PmA.74–75.
14. Pm.ii,12–13.
15. E.g. VismṬ.ii,417; DṬ.74.
16. Pm.i,58. The translation of the definition and of the following verse are based on Ven. Ñāṇamoli's rendering at Vism. XXII,115. See too Vism. XXI,11.

17. The definition is at Vism. XXII,116. For details on using the methods of the material and immaterial septads, see Vism. XX,46ff.
18. Pm.ii,63; Vism. XX,91.
19. See Chap. 6, n.15. The verse is at Pm.i,58.
20. At A.ii,92–95. See Introduction, pp.5–9.
21. Pug.61–62.
22. A.v,1–7, 311-37; S.ii,29–32.
23. SA.ii,40.
24. E.g. SA.ii,40; AA.ii,587, 676, 725.
25. For instance, at S.v,422-23 it is used to mean the Buddha's knowledge of the Four Noble Truths on the occasion of his enlightenment.
26. Vism. XXII,121.
27. Pm.i,66–67; PmA.75.
28. See e.g. MA.ii,249; Vism. VIII,235–36.
29. See e.g. A.iv,146–47.

Index

danger (*ādīnava*) 56, 60, 64, 65–66, 88, 144n.15; knowledge of 9, 31, 77, 123
death, mindfulness of (*maraṇa-sati*) 84, 110, 111
defilements (*kilesa*) 23, 79, 81, 83, 86, 87, 89, 90, 91, 94, 130n.9
delight (*nandi*) 12, 13, 50, 57, 58–60, 66–67, 88, 149n.16, 150n.25
delimitation of mind and matter (*nāmarūpa-pariccheda*) 6, 17, 30, 45, 87–88, 116, 122, 135n.8
dependent arising (*paṭicca samuppāda*) 46, 52–53, 80, 83, 131n.11
desire for deliverance (*muñcitukamyatā*) 9, 77, 91, 123, 151n.11
desireless (*appaṇihita*): contemplation 120, 136n.16; liberation 32, 83
destruction (*khaya*) 62, 63, 66, 75, 101; contemplation of 118
development (*bhāvanā*) 14, 32
Dhātuvibhaṅga Sutta 68
Dīghanakha Sutta 93–94
discernment of conditions (*paccaya-pariggaha*) 7, 19–20, 30, 56, 88, 122, 135n.11
dispassion (*virāga*) 62–63, 65, 66–69, 70–71, 82–84, 101, 145n.21, 146n.1, 146n.2, 147n.4, 147n.5, 148n.14; contemplation of 13, 63–66, 69–73, 82–84, 89, 96, 97, 98, 99, 100, 102, 147n.6, 148n.10, 148n.11, 148n.13; perception of 100, 147n.7
dissolution (*bhaṅga*) 26, 47, 62, 64, 71, 82, 88; knowledge of 9, 21–22, 31, 57, 63, 77, 82, 99, 118, 119, 151n.7, 152n.21, 153n.24
distaste for whole world (*sabbaloke anabhirata*) 100, 146n.25, 149n.15
distortion (*vipallāsa*) 23–24, 33–34, 38–39, 48, 79, 136n.19, 138n.14
doors of liberation (*vimoxkkhadvāra*) 22, 32, 48, 83, 136n.16
doubt (*vicikicchā*) 9, 46
duality 89

earth element (*paṭhavī-dhātu*) 6, 44, 55, 68, 104, 108
elements (*dhātu*) 6, 37, 44, 55, 68, 104–5, 131n.11, 142n.29, 142n.30
equanimity towards formations (*saṅkhār'upekkhā*) 9, 48, 57, 64, 69, 70, 92, 102, 122, 124
entering (*pakkhandana*) 85, 86
eternalism (*sassata-diṭṭhi*) 42, 48, 116, 141n.24
eye of Dhamma (*dhammacakkhu*) 80

faculties (*indriya*): sense 53, 54, 56, 59, 85–86, 89, 113–14, 143n.31; spiritual 22, 57, 130n.10
fall (*vaya*) 101, 119
feeling (*vedanā*) 2, 38, 41, 44, 94, 113–14, 142n.30
fetters (*saṁyojana*) 9, 115–16
fire element (*tejo-dhātu*) 44, 104–5
formations (*saṅkhārā*) 5, 15–16, 27–28, 30, 34, 48, 50, 57, 63–64, 65, 75, 77, 79, 81, 82, 83, 84, 85, 86, 87, 88, 90, 92, 94, 119, 120, 121, 123, 124, 131n.11, 135n.10, 137n.9, 144n.15; kamma- 91, 131n.11; mental 41, 114–15, 131n.11, 142n.30
foulness (*asubha*) 4, 110, 111
fruition (*phala*) 9–10, 80, 102, 132n.16
full understanding (*pariññā*) 7, 8, 10, 99, 131n.13, 135n.8

giving up (*pariccāga*) 85, 90–91, 101
gods 37–38
grasping (*ādāna*) 13, 90, 92–93

hindrances (*nīvaraṇa*) 4, 5, 87, 98, 128n.6

"I am" 39–40, 48–49, 88, 89, 92, 104–5, 140n.15, 143n.33
"I am this" 40–41, 140n.15

ignorance (*avijjā*) 2, 38, 79, 92, 105, 106, 152n.17
imagining (*maññita*) 37–42, 139n.7, 141n.27
impediments (*paḷibodha*) 3, 128n.4
impermanence (*anicca*) 7, 15–25, 26, 47, 118, 135n.10; characteristic of 15, 18–21, 31, 101, 135n.7, 135n.9, 135n.14; contemplation of 12, 13, 17, 20–22, 24, 25, 31, 63, 71, 76, 82, 88, 96, 100, 102, 118, 119, 136n.16, 145n.20; perception of 100, 134n.4, 134n.8, 157n.17
insight (*vipassanā*) 2, 5–10, 21, 31, 44, 56, 57, 67, 68, 72, 80, 86, 87, 90, 91–92, 97–98, 99, 106, 107, 116, 121, 122, 125–27, 129n.8, 130n.9; corruptions of 8, 21, 31, 108, 132n.14; eighteen 11–12, 99, 102, 117–27; into phenomena 120–21, 152n.15

jhāna 4, 110, 129n.7, 129n.8, 129n.9

kamma 86, 91
Khemaka Sutta 140n.15
knowledge, twofold 107–9

liberation (*vimokkha*) 136. *See too:* doors of liberation
loving-kindness (*mettā*) 4, 110, 111

Māgandiya 50
Māra 37, 58
matter, material form (*rūpa*) 6, 41, 42, 44, 45, 46, 47, 65, 104, 112–15, 131n.11, 136n.15, 142n.30
meditation master 3, 61, 107, 128n.3
mind, mentality (*nāma*) 6, 44, 45, 46, 105, 112–15, 131n.11, 136n.15
mind and matter (*nāmarūpa*) 30, 45, 46, 88, 104. *See too:* delimitation of mind and matter
mindfulness (*sati*): awareness and 17, 45, 46, 98, 106; four foundations of 11, 99. *See too:* breathing, mindfulness of
morality (*sīla*) 3–4

Nāgasamāla 58
Nibbāna 9–10, 25, 32, 35, 48, 57, 62, 64, 65, 75, 77, 80–81, 82, 83, 84, 86–87, 90, 91, 106, 133n.3, 147n.4, 147n.5, 147n.7, 152n.20
noble disciple 51–55, 116
non-returner (*anāgāmī*) 33, 84, 140n.15
non-self (*anattā*) 7, 36, 43, 45, 46, 47, 79, 138n.1, 138n.2; characteristic of 36, 43–44, 116; contemplation of 12, 13, 48, 93, 96, 97, 100, 102, 120, 136n.16, 143n.31; perception of 46, 49, 100, 143n.31. *See too:* self

origination (*samudaya*) 13, 26, 47, 81–83, 136n.15, 152n.21, 153n.23
overcoming doubt (*kaṅkhāvitaraṇa*) 7, 19, 46

pain 26–27, 137n.10
Pasenadi, King 67
passion (*rāga*) 13, 62, 64, 66–67, 71–72, 81, 83, 149n.16, 150n.25
path: eightfold 2; not path and 8, 122; supramundane 9, 23, 62, 64, 65, 67, 70, 75, 80–81, 86–87, 90, 97, 102, 124, 130n.9, 132n.16, 146n.1, 150n.4
Paṭisambhidāmagga 11–12, 65, 71, 82, 83, 85, 96, 97–103, 107, 112, 116, 117–27
perception (*saññā*) 41, 44, 100, 114, 126, 142n.30
permanence (*nicca*) 12, 13, 16, 23, 24
personality (*sakkāya*) 112–16; view 9, 41, 112–16, 140n.15, 140n.20, 140n.21
pleasure (*sukha*) 12, 13, 33–34
postures 29–30, 137n.10
protective meditations 4, 110–11
Puggalapaññatti 121
purifications, seven (*visuddhi*) 6–10

reflection knowledge (*paṭisaṅkhā-ñāṇa*) 9, 123
relinquishment (*paṭinissagga*) 85–87, 94, 101, 153n.4; contemplation of 13, 87, 90–93, 96, 97, 100, 102, 124, 155n.22, 156n.25
requisites of enlightenment (*bodhi-pakkhiyā dhammā*) 80
reviewing knowledge (*paccavek-khaṇa-ñāṇa*) 10, 103
revulsion (*nibbidā*) 50, 51–61, 66–69, 70, 122, 144n.1, 145n.18; contemplation of 12, 13, 56–58, 59, 60–61, 63, 64, 66, 69–70, 88, 96, 97, 102, 123; knowledge of 9, 31, 57, 64, 69, 77, 122
rise and fall (*udayabbaya*) 8, 19, 21, 31, 55, 63, 75–76, 118, 136n.15
roads to power (*iddhipāda*) 33, 138n.13
rounds, three (*tivaṭṭa*) 91

Saccaka 26
Sakka 37
saṁsāra 16, 30, 34, 80, 92, 115–16

Sāriputta 94

self (*attā*) 12, 13, 36–37, 41–42, 48, 112–16, 138n.1; perception of 37, 47, 48; view of 40–42, 48, 115–16, 140n.15, 141n.22. *See too:* non-self; personality view
serenity (*samatha*) 4, 100, 129n.8
sign (*nimitta*) 120
signless (*animitta*) 22, 84; contemplation 120, 136n.16
space element (*ākāsa-dhātu*) 105
stream-entry (*sotāpatti*) 9, 48, 116, 132n.16, 136n.19
substitution of opposites (*tadaṅga-pahāna*) 10, 23, 62, 63, 64, 71, 73, 79, 80, 86, 91, 116, 130n.9, 146n.1, 157n.17
suchness (*tathatā*) 90, 154n.13, 154n.14
suffering (*dukkha*) 2, 7, 26–28, 30, 33–34, 47, 59, 60, 92, 115–16, 137n.8, 137n.9; characteristic of 26, 29–30, 31; contemplation of 12, 13, 29, 31, 32, 48, 58, 71, 88, 93, 96, 97, 100, 102, 120, 123, 136n.16, 137n.6; perception of 34, 100, 137n.6
supramundane path. *See:* path, supramundane

triple world 25, 34, 35, 60, 77, 89, 146n.25
turning away (*vivaṭṭa*) 123–24

ultimate truth (*paramattha-sacca*) 104–6
underlying tendencies (*anusaya*) 35, 38, 48, 90, 115, 116, 130n.9, 143n.33

Vepacitti 37–38
view (*diṭṭhi*) 38, 39, 41, 48, 79, 115, 116, 138n.14, 140n.12, 141n.27, 143n.33. *See too:* personality view; self, view of
viewing, stage of 6–7, 135n.14
Visuddhimagga 12–13, 65, 91, 99, 102, 107, 117–27
voidness (*suññatā*) 48, 79, 120, 136n.16; contemplation of 121

water element (*āpo-dhātu*) 44, 104, 142n.29
wisdom 5, 79, 92, 94, 102–3, 106, 120–21. *See too:* insight meditation
worldling (*puthujjana*) 40, 115–16

Yavakalāpī Sutta 37–38, 42

THE BUDDHIST PUBLICATION SOCIETY

The BPS is an approved charity dedicated to making known the Teaching of the Buddha, which has a vital message for people of all creeds. Founded in 1958, the BPS has published a wide variety of books and booklets covering a great range of topics. Its publications include accurate annotated translations of the Buddha's discourses, standard reference works, as well as original contemporary expositions of Buddhist thought and practice. These works present Buddhism as it truly is—a dynamic force which has influenced receptive minds for the past 2500 years and is still as relevant today as it was when it first arose. A full list of our publications will be sent upon request. Write to:

The Hony. Secretary
BUDDHIST PUBLICATION SOCIETY
P.O. Box 61
54, Sangharaja Mawatha
Kandy • Sri Lanka